D1105946

Eating the
Sunrise

Christopher West

Eating the Sunrise

Meditations on the Liturgy and Our Hunger for Beauty

TOBI
PRESS

© 2023 Theology of the Body Institute Press

All rights reserved. Except for quotations, no part of this book may be reproduced or transmitted in any form or by any means, electronic or mechanical, including photocopying, recording, uploading to the internet, or by any information storage and retrieval system without written permission from the publisher.

Published by Theology of the Body Institute
PO Box 573
Quarryville, PA 17566
tobinstitute.org

ISBN: 978-1-7379945-3-4
EBook ISBN: 978-1-7379945-6-5

Printed in the United States of America

Cover design by Bill Howard, Dave Kottler, Christopher West and Juan Arreguín
Original artwork by Beth West, Instagram: @beth_rose_art
Interior Book Design by Sherry Russell

Printed by Data Reproductions Corporation, Auburn Hills, MI

First Paperback Edition

Praise for *Eating the Sunrise*

This book is not only inspired and inspiring but life-changing. West provides the "big picture" in which the Christian faith is (1) concretely embodied, (2) passionately erotic, (3) joyfully Beauty-full, and (4) mystically Eucharistic. In the process he shatters the confining little categories we are used to and replaces them with the infinitely expansive Mind of Christ. Its style is clear, accessible, and full of striking images that are sure to open the reader to the Infinite treasures of Christian liturgy.

—Peter Kreeft
Professor of Philosophy, Boston College

In this marvelous book, full of passion and poetic richness, Christopher West draws us into the mystery of the God made flesh, who has given himself to us as food—the mystery that fulfills the deepest longings of the human heart. This book will further Eucharistic revival by enkindling "Eucharistic amazement."

—Dr. Mary Healy
Professor of Scripture, Sacred Heart Major Seminary

Eating the Sunrise can bring about a needed Eucharistic Revival and along with it a revival of our humanity. By connecting the Supreme Mystery of our faith to the ache in our hearts, West helps us see how the liturgy responds to our deepest longings. Drawing extensively from the best of popes, saints, and mystics, his footnotes provide a teaching in themselves. At the same time, he warns us of other voices that have infiltrated our culture in order to corrupt our thinking and undermine our dignity. With questions for reflection and practical applications, West has provided a masterful pastoral tool that can facilitate a Eucharistic renewal in every heart and home.

—Fr. Boniface Hicks, OSB
Director of Spiritual Formation and Director of the Institute for Ministry Formation, Saint Vincent Seminary, Latrobe, PA.

For over two decades, the Church has been calling for a "New Apologetics" that responds effectively to the secularism of the modern world. While many have simply made available in new ways the "old apologetics," this book presents what the Church has been calling for. Readers will discover the insights to revive their own faith and the language to share the faith as truly good news for the modern world.

—Fr. Ryan Mann
Diocese of Cleveland

In *Eating the Sunrise*, West's beauty-forward approach explores our encounter with God in the physical world. In doing so, he offers spiritual, theological, and practical wisdom for entering the "feast of body and soul" that marks our longing for communion with God and one another. This thought-provoking book is singularly poised to facilitate Eucharistic revival.

—Christine Falk Dalessio, Ph.D.
Catholic Theology, Marquette University

Contents

To receive a PDF of a bonus chapter on the
link between sexual and liturgical chaos, visit
EatingtheSunrise.com.

Actually, We Eat It

I met a bishop some years ago who told me a story that imprinted itself on my memory.[1] He once had the opportunity to participate in a tour of a Hindu temple led by a devout Hindu woman. As they approached the central and holiest place of the temple, the woman pointed to a small structure topped by a dome and explained that a granite statue of the deity Ganesh was housed there. Recognizing a parallel to the Catholic tabernacle, the bishop asked what the structure was called. To his surprise, she said, "The sanctum sanctorum" (holy of holies).

Latin in a Hindu temple? It turns out that these Hindus employed terminology familiar to Catholics when explaining their doctrines. To his further surprise, he learned that, once the statue has been specially blessed by a Hindu priest, they believe that it is worthy of genuine worship, not mere veneration, because "Ganesh," she said, "is truly present."

He then shared that Catholics have a similar belief. "Really?" she asked. "Is that what your statues are for?" "No,"

---

1 Bishop Thomas Dowd, the former auxiliary of Montreal, and now bishop of Sault Sainte Marie, Ontario, shared this story personally with me when I was on a speaking tour in Montreal.

he replied. "Those are just reminders of Jesus or of the saints. They are not objects of worship. Our object of worship isn't made of wood or stone." "What is it made out of?" she wanted to know. "Well, food, actually." "Food?" "Yes, food. Bread and wine, to be specific."

The bishop could tell that, compared to the strong and lasting quality of granite, this Hindu woman didn't initially think that something perishable, like food, was very fitting for the divine presence. But then the possibility of an un-imagined intimacy with the deity dawned on her. "What do you *do* with this food once it has become God?" she pressed the bishop. "Actually, we eat it." "You *eat* it?" she gasped in-credulously. "Yes, we do," he affirmed. She then said with no small amount of wonder and amazement, "Well, that would make *you* the sanctum sanctorum."

CHAPTER 1

Learning to Laugh and Cry With Beauty

The origin of poetry lies in a thirst for a wilder Beauty than earth supplies.

—EDGAR ALLAN POE[1]

It's springtime as I write this, and looking out my window, I'm resisting an annual sadness that comes upon me in early May. I resist it because I don't want to be undone by something so seemingly trivial. A week ago, our redbud trees were in full bloom. Now most of their hundreds of thousands of precious pinkish-purplish petals (why they're called *red*-buds I don't know) have fallen to the ground. The fleetingness of their beauty puts a pit in my stomach.

---

1   "Horne's Orion," in *The Works of Edgar Allan Poe in Ten Volumes: Volume IV, Literary Criticism*, eds. E.C. Stedman and G.E. Woodberry (New York: Charles Scribner's Sons, 1914), 268.

Every year those brilliant dots of color try to seduce me. It's as if they want me to *feel* how drawn I am to their beauty. But I've learned not to fall for it. I'll give their calling colors a quick nod, a minimal acknowledgment ("Aren't they pretty?"), but part of me doesn't want to let the beauty *in*. Part of me doesn't actually want to feel it. Because if I *feel* it, then I have to face my waking aching—that painful cry of my heart for . . . for . . . *for what?!*

It's a critical question. In fact, the very first thing we hear from the mouth of Jesus in the Gospel of John is an invitation to probe that ache: "*What do you want?*" Or sometimes rendered as, "*What are you looking for?*" (Jn 1:38). If I pay my waking aching a little attention, it becomes pretty obvious what it wants: it wants *a beauty that lasts!* It wants—even more, it demands—a beauty that never fades, a beauty that doesn't die. It wants a beauty whose promise of delight is certain and secure, without fear of loss or disappointment. It wants an ever-flowing river of beauty that I can drink in unto infinite satisfaction. A bold desire, I know. But, as I really look at the cry of my heart, honesty demands such boldness. *That's* what I want.

The beauty of those redbud trees can awaken that yearning in me, but—and here's where that annual sadness comes from—their fleeting beauty *cannot possibly satisfy it.* So part of me would rather keep the ache safely tucked in under the covers, asleep. Because when the ache is awake, I break. I split open. I'm undone. I pine for an infinite beauty that no finite beauty can satisfy. And to pine like that is *painful!*

Learning to Laugh with the Sacraments

I've come to discover that right there—*in* the pain of the pining for beauty—is a lesson in anthropology, cosmology, and theology (who/what is man, the universe, God?) as potent as all the lessons contained in all the tomes ever written on those subjects.

Right there—*in* the thirst for infinite beauty—we've stumbled upon the very essence of what makes a human being unique among all the creatures of the world.[2] Animals may have some sensate attraction to bright colors and shapely forms, but they don't pine for everlasting beauty; they don't look up at the stars and wonder what's out there; they don't get in a knot over the allure of redbud trees. Why does beauty do that to us? What *is* beauty to begin with? The young, future John Paul II affirms that it's "difficult to answer that question. Everything that is beautiful draws us to itself. It delights us," he observes. "There is a certain unique sensitivity to beauty in the human soul, a kind of musical string that vibrates when a person meets up with beauty. Beauty delights and attracts. And because it attracts, this indicates that there is something else beyond it, which is hidden."[3] And here we glimpse the deepest truth and meaning of the cosmos: its essential truth is its sacramentality—its ability to symbolize and communicate the absolute Beauty that lies beyond it. We can all observe, says Karol Wojtyla, that "beauty is abundantly, superabundantly, distributed throughout the visible world. But indeed, in this dispersion of beauty, no beauty is beautiful in an absolute sense. God alone is absolute Beauty."[4]

---

2   As Pope Benedict XVI put it, "The thirst for the infinite belongs quite simply to essential human nature." Then he goes even further and affirms that this thirst "is indeed precisely that essential nature" (*The Yes of Jesus Christ* [New York: Crossroad Publishing, 2016], 11).

3   Karol Wojtyla, *God Is Beauty: A Retreat on the Gospel and Art* (TOB Institute Press, 2021), 25.

4   Ibid, 4.

And at this point we've arrived at our theology lesson. The biblical message, contrary to what many suppose it to be, is that God wants to quench our thirst for infinite Beauty by himself becoming blissfully delightful wine poured out for us to drink unto endless intoxication. *That's* the good news of the Gospel: there is a wine that can truly quench our thirst for the infinite, and it's freely poured out for us in the Church's liturgy! "The King seems to refuse nothing to the Bride!" exclaims Saint Teresa of Avila in her reflection on the biblical image of being invited to God's wine cellar.[5] "Well, then, let her drink as much as she desires and get drunk on all these wines in the cellar of God! Let her enjoy these joys, wonder at these great things, and not fear to lose her life through drinking much more than her weak nature enables her to do. Let her die at last in this paradise of delights; blessed death that makes one live in such a way."[6]

An experience such as this is the fruit of a contemplative way of seeing the world. The Latin *com* + *templum* means roughly "to see within the temple"—to see the world *as* a temple, if you will; to see all things in a sacred light. "I hold that this is the specific mark of seeing things in contemplation," says Catholic philosopher Josef Pieper: "It is motivated by loving acceptance, by an affectionate affirmation." He goes on to explain the fruit of such "seeing" by appealing to the German expression *sich nicht satt sehen können*, which means one "can't see enough" of something. "In one respect," he says, this "indicates utmost delight: thus new parents 'can't see enough' of their baby. But then it also means that the desire to

---

5   "Wine cellar" is sometimes rendered "banquet hall" in Song of Songs 2:4.
6   Teresa of Avila, *Meditations on the Song of Songs*, Chapter 6.

'see enough' is never satisfied. In this craving to 'see' there is a dimension that . . . always remains unfulfilled!" Commenting on Catholic poet Konrad Weiss's remark that "contemplation will not be satisfied until blinded by the object of its ultimate desires," Pieper concludes: "Such a statement almost leads us beyond the confines of this world."[7]

Yes, that's what contemplation does. It enables one to recognize all that is true, good, and beautiful in this world—from redbud trees to supernovas, from butterflies to buffalos, from wine itself to the wonder of the human body—as so many signs of ultimate Truth, Goodness, and Beauty. Even more, in and through contemplation, these signs "split open" and spill their divine secrets.[8] Contemplation demonstrates that one has gained a "divine sense of humor" and is able to laugh with the sacraments that are all around us. Bishop Fulton J. Sheen explains as follows:

> A person is said to have a sense of humor if he can "see through" things; one lacks a sense of humor if he cannot "see through" things. . . . Our Lord had a divine sense of humor, because he revealed that the universe was sacramental. A sacrament, in a very broad sense of the term, combines two elements: one visible, the other invisible—one that can be seen, or tasted, or touched, or heard; the other unseen to the eyes of the flesh. There is, however, some kind of relation or significance between the two. A spoken word is a kind of sacrament, because there is something material or audible about it; there is also something spiritual about it,

---

7   Josef Pieper, *Only the Love Sings: Art and Contemplation* (Ignatius Press, 1990), 75–76.

8   See Jean Corbon, *The Wellspring of Worship* (Ignatius Press, 1988), 136.

namely, its meaning. A horse can hear a funny story just as well as a man. It is conceivable that the horse may hear the words better than the man and at the end of the story the man may laugh, but the horse will never give a horse laugh. The reason is that the horse gets only the material side of the "sacrament," namely, the sound; but the man gets the invisible or the spiritual side, namely, the meaning.[9]

Those redbud trees are a kind of sacrament. There's a divine message, a hidden *meaning* within every one of those hundreds of thousands of pinkish-purplish petals to which we, as incarnate-spirits, have access. Right at the start of the Bible we read that "the Lord God made various trees grow that were delightful to look at" (Gen 2:9), and Jesus himself, interestingly enough, invites us to ponder what the trees are trying to tell us when their buds burst open (see Lk 21:29–31). There's a promise of eternal fulfillment foreshadowed in the beauty of creation. The Eastern Church calls this experience of glimpsing uncreated Beauty via created beauty *theophany* (*theos-phainein* in Greek means "to show God").[10] It's a word that opens us to everything for which we yearn, so we'll be unfolding and returning to it throughout this book.

Saint Augustine invites us to the experience of theophany with this challenge: "Question the beauty of the earth, question the beauty of the sea, . . . question the beauty of the sky . . . question all these realities. All respond: 'See, we are beautiful.' Their beauty is a profession. These beauties are subject to change. Who made them if not the Beautiful One who is not subject to

---

9 Fulton Sheen, *These Are the Sacraments* (Image, 1964), 11–12.
10 *Theos*, Greek for "God," comes from the verb *theaomai*, which means "I watch" or "I see."

change?"[11] The fact that the beauties of the world are subject to change—and are, thus, fleeting—can make us sad indeed. But that sadness can also open us to the hope of participating in the Life of the Beautiful One who is not subject to change. Our highest pleasures in the beauties of this temporal world "are only shadows of eternal joy," says Caryll Houselander. And if our minds are "illuminated by the ray of the divine light," we will know "in every passing, simple happiness, in the brief loveliness of the senses . . . the eternal now."[12]

Such knowledge, however, is not automatic, and that means learning to laugh with the sacramentality of the world presents a task and a challenge. These "eternal nows" provided by the "brief loveliness of the senses" whisper to us of lasting Beauty, but only for an instant. In this world we must suffer the ache of longing for the Infinite without demanding more from the finite than it can offer. When we shut down our hearts and refuse to *feel*—because we don't want to endure the pain of pining—we inevitably trade in that suffering for another: a dehumanizing condition called *equi oblivione* (a horse's obliviousness, as Fulton Sheen might describe it).

Learning to Weep with the Sacraments

Someone with an aesthetic sensibility is particularly aware of and drawn to the beautiful. When we shut down our hearts, we become anesthetized (an-aesthetic = "numb to beauty"). Jesus calls it "hardness of heart" and laments: "We played the flute for you, but you did not dance. We sang a dirge, but you did not weep" (Lk 7:32). To such as these, "this world is

---

11   Cited in *Catechism of the Catholic Church* (henceforth CCC) 32.
12   Caryll Houselander, *Mother of Christ* (Sheed and Ward, 1978), 49.

opaque like a curtain; nothing can be seen through it," says Sheen. A redbud tree in full bloom is just a redbud tree in full bloom. No deeper meaning can be discerned. But to those who *see* and those who *feel*, "to poets, artists, and saints, the world is transparent like a window pane—it tells of something beyond."[13] To those who *see* and *feel*, everything becomes an occasion of *theophany*.

Year after year those redbud trees in my yard sing to me, attempting to woo me into the divine sense of humor. They want to open my eyes and my heart to the lasting Beauty signified by their fleeting beauty, and give me a little taste of it even here and now. Those blooming buds whisper to me: "You will not be unhappy; the desire of your heart will be fulfilled, what is more, it is already being fulfilled."[14] But if I'm to learn to laugh with the sacramentality of those shimmering colors (to delight in them, yes, but more so, to delight in what they point to; to rejoice in their promise), I have to learn to weep with them, too. As Joseph Ratzinger (the future Benedict XVI) observed, we all experience that "primordial sensation which Nietzsche expressed in the words, 'All joy wills eternity, wills deep, deep eternity.' . . . What is glimpsed in [some moments] should never end. That it *does* end . . . is the real sadness of human existence."[15] If I really want to experience the full joy of laughing with those redbud trees, I have to learn how to embrace that annual sadness they visit upon me: be willing to *feel* it; be willing to let it undo me, without shutting it down.

---

13 Sheen, *These Are the Sacraments*, 11.
14 John Paul II, Letter addressing the *Communion and Liberation* gathering in Rimini, Italy, August 2002.
15 Joseph Ratzinger, *Eschatology* (Catholic University of America Press, 1988), 94.

The sorrowful mysteries of the Christian life precede the glorious mysteries: "Happy are you who weep . . . for you will laugh" (Lk 6:21). "Your pain will turn into joy" (Jn 16:20). Weeping and laughing, pain and joy, dying and rising are written into creation itself. If I want to pass over to the lasting Beauty and fulfillment to which those precious petals point, like them, *I* must be willing to fall to the ground and die (see Jn 12:24). *That's* the part I don't like. *That's* the part I resist. My redbud trees are inviting me to embrace another far more mysterious and far more agonizing tree: the Cross. That which is fearful and self-preserving in me would prefer a fulfillment, a beauty, a theophany without the Cross; the joy without the pain; the ecstasy without the agony; the laughter without the weeping.

It sounds desirable, but for the fact that it's an illusion. As we'll discuss at more length in the final chapter, there's no detour around the Cross. And to the degree that we discover the Cross as *the way* to the glory we desire—"we suffer with him so that we may also be glorified with him" (Rom 8:17)—we can make sense out of why the saints even come to embrace their suffering. For example, Saint Faustina, having been granted a glimpse of the degrees of glory that await us on the other side, exclaimed: "O my God, if I were thereby able to attain one more degree [of glory], I would gladly suffer all the torments of the martyrs put together. Truly, all those torments seem as nothing to me compared with the glory that is awaiting us for all eternity."[16] Please ponder this: what kind of *sheer ecstasy*, what kind of *everlasting glory* must she have glimpsed that would cause her to utter such madness?

16 Saint Maria Faustina Kowalska, *Diary* 605.

Liturgy Reorients our Desire

"The fascination of beauty is the only way to educate the person for the Future," writes Stanislaw Grygiel[17] (the capital F signifying one's *ultimate* future/destiny). "There is no other way to educate the human person, for he belongs to beauty."[18] What we learn along the way of this education can be summed up in these three points:

1. we are made to slake our thirst at the fountain of infinite Beauty;
2. finite beauty is but a sign (theophany) of infinite Beauty;
3. and to reach that everlasting Beauty, we must pass over from the sign to the reality signified via a painful dying that promises a glorious rising again.

This painful dying and rising involves a reeducation of the heart in regard to what it treasures. The things we treasure on earth are fleeting: they're subject to the destruction of moths and decay and threatened by thieves, as Jesus reminds us. But Christ also speaks of a lasting treasure that moths, decay, and thieves cannot touch, and he invites us to redirect our hearts there (see Mt 6:19–21). This is what embracing a sacramental vision—which is to say an authentically Christian and liturgical vision—of the world entails. We don't come to

17 Stanislaw Grygiel was a longtime friend of Karol Wojtyla, under whose direction Grygiel wrote his doctoral dissertation. In the early years of his pontificate, John Paul II called Grygiel to Rome to serve as a professor at his newly established Institute for Studies on Marriage and Family. I had the pleasure of studying under Grygiel in the mid-1990s when he visited the American branch of the John Paul II Institute.
18 Stanislaw Grygiel, *Discovering the Human Person in Conversation with John Paul II* (Eerdmans, 2014), 125.

appreciate the things of this world *less*; we come to appreciate them even *more*, because we appreciate them rightly as signs of the divine promise that our hunger for lasting Beauty *will* be satisfied. We appreciate them without clinging to them, without demanding that they satisfy our yearning for the infinite: "I treasure your promise in my heart, lest I sin against you" (Ps 119:11).

We sin against the Lord whenever we expect something that is *not* God to be what only God can be for us: the satisfaction of our hunger for everlasting Beauty. Christian liturgy, when we allow it to have its way with us, reorients our desire toward its only true fulfillment. We will have more to say about liturgy as these meditations unfold, but let's begin with a basic definition. As the *Catechism* explains, "The word 'liturgy' originally meant a 'public work' or a 'service in the name of/on behalf of the people.' In Christian tradition it means the participation of the People of God in 'the work of God.'"[19] The work of God, says Jesus, is to "believe in the one he sent"—to believe that Jesus is God's eternal Son, sent by the Father as "bread from heaven" to satisfy our hunger for absolute Beauty (see Jn 6:29–33). This is God's gift to our insatiably hungry hearts, the gift we receive in the liturgy. Christians claim to believe in such a God—a God who makes of *himself* a gift we can take *into* ourselves unto infinite satisfaction. But do we *really* believe? To the degree that we find ourselves either attempting to squash our deepest longings or attempting to satisfy them by aiming them at the visible, tangible, and fleeting pleasures of this world, we aren't living from faith in such a God.

19 CCC 1069.

Paraphrasing an illuminating passage from Benedict XVI's prepapal book *Introduction to Christianity*, to say "I believe in God" signifies not the observation of this or that fact but a fundamental mode of behavior toward existence, toward reality as a whole. It signifies the deliberate view that what cannot be seen represents true reality, that at the very core of human existence we find a hunger that cannot finally be nourished by the visible and tangible. Such an attitude can be attained only by what the Bible calls "conversion." Our center of gravity draws us to the visible, to what we can take in our hands and hold as our own. Hence, we are in need of an inward turnaround if we are to see how badly we are neglecting our own fulfillment by trusting only what we see with our eyes. Without this change of direction there can be no belief. Indeed, belief *is* the conversion in which we discover that we are following an illusion if we devote ourselves only to the tangible. And because our center of gravity does not cease to incline us in the other direction, the need for conversion is new every day. Only in a lifelong conversion, Ratzinger concludes, can we become aware of what it means to say "I believe in God."[20]

Our Hunger Has a Name

This hunger we find at the core of our humanity "is of divine origin," as the *Catechism* affirms. "God has placed it in the human heart in order to draw man to the One who alone can fulfill it."[21] But what are we to call that hunger? The Church borrows her language here from the Greeks and calls it, rather surprisingly to many, *eros* (from which we derive the word

---

20 See Ratzinger, *Introduction to Christianity* (Ignatius Press, 1990), 24-25.
21 CCC 1718.

"erotic"). If we are to understand *eros* correctly, however, we must never confuse it with another Greek word, *porneia*. The pornographic culture in which we live has grievously bastardized the erotic. We make a tragic and heart-crushing mistake when we confuse these gross distortions of *eros* with *eros* itself, as if the erotic realm were perverse at its roots. As the ancient mystical writer Dionysius the Areopagite reminds us, "Eros has its primal roots in the beautiful and the good: eros exists and comes into being only through the beautiful and good."[22]

Let us hold on firmly to this basic principle of Catholic cosmology: *The devil doesn't have his own clay.* All he can do is take *God's* clay—all of which is "very good" (Gen 1:31)—and twist it, distort it. The good news is that Christ came into the world to untwist the clay that sin and the devil twisted up. While our understanding of eros is badly in need of rehabilitation, the good news, as papal preacher Raniero Cardinal Cantalamessa reminds us, is that Christ has "come to save the world, beginning with eros, which is the dominant force."[23] *Salvation begins with eros!* What a remarkable assertion (and not one I ever heard growing up in Catholic schools). The tragedy of our fallen world is that the sacred has been desecrated. The good news of salvation is that the desecrated can be re-consecrated (made sacred again)[24]—and it all begins with eros.

I often say that God gave us eros to be like the fuel of a rocket with enough combustible force to launch us to the stars.

22   Dionysius the Areopagite, *The Divine Names*, 4.13.
23   Raniero Cantalamessa, "The Two Faces of Love," First Lenten Sermon to the Roman Curia, 2011.
24   This verbiage is borrowed with gratitude from my friend and colleague Jeanette Clark. See her presentation "Nuptial Spirituality and the Present Moment" at tobvirtualconference.com.

But there's an enemy who doesn't want us to reach those stars, so his goal is to invert the engines of our desire. The word "desire" itself comes from the Latin *de sidere*, meaning "from the stars," or "to await what the stars may bring." When desire becomes inverted, it is literally *disastrous*: a turning away (*dis*) from the stars (*astrum*, another Latin word for "the stars"). This is our fallen condition: we're made for the Infinite, but we cling dis-astrously to the finite. The good news is that "conversion," as we described it above, is truly possible. The Infinite One himself has entered this finite world not to condemn our dis-astrous lives; rather, he came to redirect our rocket engines toward the stars! And in launching with him, we leave nothing that is true, good, and beautiful in this world behind. Christ's *bodily ascension* into the infinite realm assures us that the entire physical world is destined in some way to be divinized!

Those who reap the fruits of this redemption of eros (a lifelong endeavor involving continual dying and rising) rediscover that erotic longing, in its richest sense, is a reaching and a yearning with every fiber of our being for the fullness of life, the fullness of love, the fullness of God. They rediscover—or perhaps discover for the first time—that, contrary to widespread (mis)understanding, Christ does not want us to repress or annihilate eros. In the words of John Paul II, Christ wants us to experience the "fullness of 'eros,'" which implies the upward impulse of the human spirit toward what is true, good, and beautiful, so that what is 'erotic' also becomes true, good, and beautiful."[25]

Some have characterized *eros* as a selfish or even base love and *agape* as the more sacrificial and, therefore, Christian

---

25 John Paul II, *Man and Woman He Created Them: A Theology of the Body* (Henceforth, TOB) (Boston: Pauline, 2006) 48:1.

form of love. But this, once again, is to confuse *eros* with *porneia*. As we allow grace to "redirect our rocket engines," eros becomes the open channel of the human heart through which we express agape.[26] True eros, therefore, leads not to the base and the pornographic. Rather, as Benedict XVI expresses it, rightly directed eros "leads to being drawn out and finding oneself before the mystery that encompasses the whole of existence." It "becomes a pilgrimage . . . toward authentic self-discovery and indeed the discovery of God." The pilgrimage of eros, he concludes, "is not, then, about suffocating the longing that dwells in the heart of man, but about freeing it, so that it can reach its true height."[27]

What is that true height? In the words of Saint Francis de Sales, eros is the desire in us that "passionately rushes toward divinization."[28] *Divinization*: to participate in the everlasting Beauty of the divine Life, the divine Ecstasy, the divine exchange of Love among the eternal Persons of the Trinity: this is the true height to which eros is meant to launch us; this is the definitive goal of human life, to become "partakers of the divine nature" (2 Pt 1:4). "Ah! What a union of our hearts there shall be with God there above in heaven," exclaims de Sales. He continues by explaining that, in eternity,

after these infinite desires of the true good never assuaged in this world, we shall find the living and powerful source

---

26 See Pope Benedict XVI's encyclical *God Is Love* for an extensive treatment of the relationship between *eros* and *agape*. See also my book unpacking that encyclical, *The Love That Satisfies: Reflections on Eros and Agape*.

27 Benedict XVI, "The Year of Faith. The Desire for God," General Audience Address of November 7, 2012.

28 Abbe Jacques Leclercq, *Saint Francois de Sales, Docteur de la Perfection* (Gabriel Basuchesne, 1928), 103.

thereof. Then, truly, as we see a hungry child closely fixed to his mother's breast, greedily press this dear fountain of most desired sweetness, so that one would think that either it would thrust itself into its mother's breast, or else suck and draw all that breast into itself; so our soul, panting with an extreme thirst for the true good, when she shall find that inexhaustible source in the Divinity—O Good God! what a holy and sweet ardor to be united and joined to the plentiful breasts of the All-goodness, either to be altogether absorbed in it, or have it come entirely into us![29]

Scripture itself speaks of heaven as the experience of sucking deeply from the abundant breasts of the New Jerusalem and finding comfort and delight in the overflow of her milk (see Is 66:10–11). The dim glimpse of such heavenly satisfaction and bliss is what led Saint Faustina to exclaim that she would gladly suffer all the torments of the martyrs put together to gain one more degree of this glory—yet I'm unwilling to suffer the loss of those beautiful blossoms on my redbud trees? Lord, open my eyes to the joys on the other side of embracing the losses in my life!

INTO THE MYSTIC

1. What's something you learned in this chapter that you hadn't known before?

2. What experiences of beauty bring about the waking of your aching? In other words, where do you experience

---

29 Francis de Sales, *Treatise on the Love of God* (Catholic Way Publishing, 2015), 218.

theophanies? Do you find yourself willing to "suffer the ache," or are you inclined to ignore or suppress it?

3. Does the idea that you are made to slake your thirst at an infinite fountain of Beauty ring true to your experience? Is this what you've understood the Christian Faith to hold out to you? Does it sound like a fantasy? Do you believe that God actually wants to satisfy that thirst?

4. What's your honest reaction to hearing that our thirst for Infinite Beauty is properly called *eros*? In what ways has your understanding of "erotic longing" been desecrated? How do you imagine that it can be reconsecrated (made sacred again)? Do you believe that reconsecration is possible?

CHAPTER 2

You Don't Have to Eat Like a Bird

Love is strong as death
Longing is fierce . . .
Its arrows are arrows of fire
Flames of the divine.

—SONG OF SONGS 8:6

In the above passage from the Song of Songs—that great erotic love poetry of Sacred Scripture—the human heart cries out for a love that is strong as death. Commenting on this passage, Joseph Ratzinger explains that the "boundless demands of *eros* . . . give expression to a basic problem, indeed *the* basic problem, of human existence." It is this: the heart "demands infinity but cannot grant it; . . . it claims eternity but in fact is included in the world of death, in its loneliness and its power of destruction."[1]

---

1   Ratzinger, *Introduction to Christianity*, 230.

Let's pause to ponder that for a moment. It's another re-markable assertion: *the* basic problem of human existence—of your life and mine—is found in *the cry of eros*. Really? Isn't the basic problem just survival, finding some way to put food in our bellies? Ah, yes. When we start right there with the basic desire for survival—for food—we stumble once again upon the sacramentality of the world. Food, and our need for it, is a sign to which we must pay very careful attention—a sign we must contemplate until it splits open and spills its heavenly secrets.

The Sacredness of Eating

Those who have never lacked access to food tend to take eating for granted. We do it out of habit and forget the fun-damental fact that we eat because we want to live. "Is there anything more basic than that?" my professor and mentor, the late Monsignor Lorenzo Albacete, used to ask.[2] Eating is the condition for everything else. Our need for food also re-veals our dependency, our vulnerability: we are *not* self-suf-ficient; life is fragile. The threat of our existence being taken away, the threat of life ending, looms heavily on the horizon. Eating is a reminder of that. In fact, although we don't tend to think much about it, whenever we eat, we are absorbing the life of some plant or animal which had to die in order for us to live.

When food is plentiful and chicken breasts come skinned, deboned, and frozen in a ziplocked bag, we can easily become

---

2 Lorenzo Albacete was a personal friend of John Paul II; he had charged Albacete with helping to establish the American branch of the Pontifical Institute for Studies on Marriage and Family. Various themes that follow were gleaned from Monsignor Albacete's *Retrieve* video series, episode 2 (Life After Sunday, 1994), lifeaftersunday.com/purification-stage/videos.

oblivious to the profundity and sacredness of a meal—to the fact that living and dying and eating are inextricably intertwined. Whenever we eat, we are saying: I want my life to go on. We are saying: I don't want to die. And, I'd suggest, we should be giving thanks (Greek, *eucharistia*) for whatever living thing was sacrificed so that our life *can* go on.

While reflecting on the lost sense of the sacredness of eating, Monsignor Albacete would invite his students to consider the frantic and threatened manner in which birds eat. I think of seagulls fighting and squawking over scraps of food stolen from distracted beachgoers—sometimes right out of their hands! We may be more civilized about it, but we, too, have a bit of that mentality when we eat (just think of the internal battle you face when someone asks for a bite of that last serving of dessert you'd been hiding for yourself in the back of the fridge).

We tend to eat like birds because, well, food is finite. We want a satisfaction of our hunger that is not threatened by insecurity, by finiteness—which is to say, we want a food (if such were to exist) that promises *infinite satisfaction*. And this brings us back to the basic problem of human existence: the hunger and thirst of eros demands infinity but cannot grant it. This "takes us directly to the heart of Christianity," says Benedict XVI. He continues:

> The Infinite itself, in fact, to make himself a response that man might experience, assumed a finite form. From the . . . moment when the Word became flesh, he eliminated the unbridgeable distance between the finite and the infinite: the eternal and infinite God left his heaven and entered into time, he immersed himself in human finitude. Nothing,

35

then, is banal or insignificant along the path of life and of the world. Man is made for an infinite God who became flesh, who assumed our humanity in order to draw us to the heights of his divine being.[3]

Hunger and Thirst Will Be Holy

And how does he draw us to the heights of his divine being? Through hunger and thirst. Through eating and drinking. In the liturgy, humble bread and humble wine become the grandest theophany, become divine! The following poem, which I've adapted slightly from Father Harry Cronin, expresses this mystery exquisitely:

The Mass is a poem written with the blood of God:
written after that bright time when we knew with certainty
that God had a body and hands and a voice
to announce his love.

Christ is a determined and deliberate lover.
And this loving is done with bread.
He loves in bread and wine.

For the dimmest fool will know
that bread and wine are for hunger and thirst.
And if hunger is fed with this bread,
and thirst is slaked with this wine
then hunger and thirst for us will be holy.

---

3   Benedict XVI, Letter addressing the *Communion and Liberation* gathering in Rimini, Italy, August 10, 2012.

For hunger and thirst, basic and brutal,
will gently jostle us toward the embrace of God.
It is blunt and simple.
It needs only careful, clear telling.
Our God in Christ has become food
because our God in Christ knows inside his own flesh
every sad, tear-filled tale of hunger and thirst.

He knows that the greatest hungering ache
is the hungering for our beginning:
for that crack of love's lightning
that shot us into being.

Which we find only in bread . . .[4]

It is blunt and simple, basic and brutal: we eat because we want to live. And if such were to exist, we would want a food that is "strong as death." In fact, we would want a food that is *stronger than death*. And the utterly astonishing claim of Christianity is that there *is* such a food!

I am the living bread that came down from heaven; whoever eats this bread will live forever; and the bread that I will give is my flesh for the life of the world. . . . Amen, amen, I say to you, unless you eat the flesh of the Son of Man and drink his blood, you do not have life within you. Whoever eats my flesh and drinks my blood has eternal life, and I will raise him on the last day. For my flesh is true food, and my

4   Adapted from the "Meditation of the Day" by Father Harry Cronin in *Magnificat*, May 5, 2000.

blood is true drink. . . . This is the bread that came down from heaven. Unlike your ancestors who ate and still died, whoever eats this bread will live forever. (Jn 6:51–58)

"Why should we be surprised that he gives himself to us as food?" asks Fulton Sheen. "After all, if he furnishes food for the birds and the beasts in the natural order, why should he not furnish it for man in the supernatural order?" The natural order is a theophany, a revelation of God: "Running through the universe is the law that nothing lives unless it consumes," Sheen observes. By this law we learn that "the joy of living comes from communion with another kind of life." Sheen muses that "if the chemical could speak, it would say to the plant: 'Unless you eat me, you shall not have life in you.' If the plant could speak, it would say to the animal: 'Unless you eat me, you shall not have life in you.' If the animal, plant, and air could speak they would say to man: 'Unless you eat me, you shall not have life in you.'" Sheen then concludes, "If the plant nourishes its seed before it is ripe, and if the bird brings food to its young before they can fly, shall we deny to [the Creator] that which we allow to a creature? To every infant at the breast the mother virtually says: 'Take, eat and drink; this is my body and blood.'"[5]

Digestion and Divinization

Two thousand years later the response to Jesus's teaching on the Eucharist is, understandably, the same: "How can this man give us his flesh to eat? . . . This is a hard teaching; who can accept it?" (Jn 6:52, 60). But, once again, if we look at

5   Sheen, *These Are the Sacraments*, 77, 78, 79.

nature's theology lessons, maybe it isn't so hard after all to believe that bread and wine can become the Body and Blood of Jesus. Has it ever dawned on you that whenever Jesus ate bread and drank wine, they became his body and blood through the natural process of digestion? Saint Gregory of Nyssa observed that whatever bread Jesus ate "was thereby raised to divine power," adding that "a similar change happens to the bread of the Eucharist."[6]

Ponder this for a moment (or more!): if Jesus is who he said he was, then in his body digestion was the divinization of *everything* he ate and drank. If the goal of creation is that all things would be summed up in Christ, that all would become one in him, divinized in him (see Eph 1:10; Rom 8:21–23),[7] how happy was Mary to give the Christ Child her breast and its flow of milk?! How happy were the nuts and the figs and the fish that Jesus ate?! Did they not consider it the utmost privilege to be chosen as food for their Creator? "Please, you're so beautiful. You may eat me if you like," says the mare Hwin to Aslan in *The Chronicles of Narnia*.[8]

Might we view the words of consecration ("This is my body. . . . This is my blood") as a kind of *supernatural* fulfillment of the

---

6 Gregory of Nyssa, *Catechetical Oration* 37, as cited in Olivier Clement, *The Roots of Christian Mysticism* (New City Press, 1993), 110.

7 Scott Hahn makes the point that the biblical idea of the earth having "four corners" (see Isa 11:12; Rev 7:1) does not indicate an antiquated belief in a flat earth. Rather, the biblical authors saw the earth as an altar. Then Hahn proposes that, when Christ returns, "he will put his hands over the altar of the earth and say, 'This is my Body.' But this time it won't be bread and wine transubstantiated. It will be the heavens and the earth" (*Hope to Die*, [Emmaus Road Publishing, 2020], 85).

8 C.S. Lewis, *The Horse and His Boy*, in *The Chronicles of Narnia*, complete set (Harper Collins, 2001), 299 (my thanks to David Fagerberg for pointing this out in his book *Liturgical Mysticism* [Emmaus Academic, 2019], 11).

natural reality of Jesus's digestion of bread and wine? The point here is not to banalize the Mass, nor to reduce the doctrine of transubstantiation (the technical term for the transformation of bread and wine into the sacrament of Christ's Body and Blood) to a merely biological process. Rather, the point is to recognize the extra-ordinary in the ordinary—that is the sacramental life! The point is to illuminate the mystery of the Eucharist as the superabounding sacramental re-presentation of the total reality and mystery of the Incarnation, of the Word made flesh. We've grown so accustomed to the expression "Word made flesh" that we're no longer astonished by "God's colossal synthesis of seemingly unbridgeable divisions." We need to rediscover this marriage of heaven and earth as "something altogether new and foreign to every history and to all cultures." This is something we can enter into "in faith and only in faith." And "when we do, it opens up to us wholly new horizons of thought and life."[9]

One of the doorways in to these new horizons is through the Greek word *Logos*. English doesn't have an equivalent for *Logos*—translated "Word." The Greek *Logos* refers to the meaning, the logic, the reason, the purpose behind and within all things. To say the Word became flesh is to say that *Ultimate Meaning* became flesh; and to take on flesh is to take on the entire mystery of the physical universe. If the *Logos*—the Logic and Reason behind all things—was truly born of a woman, truly took on human flesh, truly hungered and thirsted as we do, ate and drank as we do, digested food and drink as we do, *then the biological has become theological.*[10] If the Incarnation is real, then *nothing is banal*, as Pope Benedict XVI says above.

---

9   Joseph Ratzinger, *Mary: The Church at the Source* (Ignatius Press, 1995), 90.
10   See ibid, 33.

For both Jesus and us, digestion is mysteriously intertwined with divinization, although in different ways. In Jesus, digesting bread and wine divinizes them: the bread and wine become his Body and Blood. In us, digesting his Body and Blood, in the appearance of bread and wine, divinizes us.[11] We are what we eat. Or, as one of the Church's prayers after communion has it, we are "transformed into what we consume."

To sum up, in Jesus's bread of life discourse, it would seem he is saying: "Do not be incredulous when I affirm that the fruit of the earth and of the vine can become my Body and Blood. I have entered this earth and this earth has entered me. Every Mass is the sacramental re-presentation of this mystery. The bread and wine I ate and drank among you, which became my Body and Blood, I now re-present to you to eat and drink in this Sacred Sacrament. I have divinized them by digesting them, and if you now digest them, they will divinize you!"

Something about the visceralness of all this can cause us to recoil. When the implications of a God-in-the-flesh become challenging, even scandalous, we opt for a "sort of" incarnate Christ, or even an excarnate Christ. Let's face it, a Jesus who loves and nourishes us only "spiritually" is much more tenable (and much more becoming!) than a Jesus who literally *bleeds* to love us and, even more, wants to mingle his flesh and blood with our digestive juices.

But Jesus isn't scandalized by eating and drinking and digestive juices. He invented them! And not just so we could enjoy a good cheeseburger (as wonderful as that can be). He

---

11 A similar distinction is revealed when we compare the Lord's baptism to ours. When we were baptized, the waters sanctified us. But this is only possible because when Christ was baptized he sanctified the waters.

invented them, as we are coming to discover, so that his eternal divine joy might be *in* us and our joy might be complete (see Jn 15:11). He invented eating and drinking and digestive juices so we could be divinized by feeding on him (see Jn 6:57). The Greek verb in John 6:54 (*trogon*) is very specific on this point: Christ is inviting all those who hunger for eternal life to "gnaw" on his flesh.[12]

Hope of Satisfying Eros

All of this means that this "true food" and "true drink" (Jn 6:55), gnawed on and swallowed and digested by *the body*, has the ability somehow to reach the deeper hunger and thirst of *the spirit*. In one of her prayers over the offerings at Mass, the Church praises God for meeting "the twofold needs of human nature" in the Eucharistic bread and wine and asks "that the sustenance they provide may not fail us in body or in spirit." It is an astounding testimony to the humility of God that he chooses to reach our most intimate depths through a small, edible fragment of matter. Herein we encounter the culmination of the mystery of the Incarnation.[13] Ah, the mysterious wedding of the visible and the invisible! The physical and the spiritual! *That* is the Eucharist! In this most glorious Sacrament, our bodies are nourished with food

---

12 While John's Gospel is underscoring the fact of Christ's Real Presence in the Eucharist with the Greek word *trogon*, the Church does not hold that we chew on the Lord's flesh as cannibals would do. "Jesus is not there like a piece of meat," observes Ratzinger. Rather, the substance of the bread and of the wine "is transformed, that is to say, the fundamental basis of its being. That is what is at stake, and not the superficial category, to which everything we can measure or touch belongs" (*God Is Near Us: The Eucharist, the Heart of Life* [Ignatius Press, 2001], 85).

13 See Pope Francis, *Laudato Si* 236.

and our souls are nourished with the living hope that the unsatisfiable cry of eros will not go unsatisfied. This living hope of satisfaction, in turn, becomes the very life force of one's faith. Without it, "our desire becomes infuriating and our faith grows weak," as Saint Hilary observes,[14] because the basic problem of human existence—our yearning for infinite satisfaction—seems unsolvable.

The basic problem of *human eros* is solved by opening to the infilling of *divine eros*. This is what happens in the Eucharist (at least, it's what's *meant* to happen). Here we discover that Christ "is a lover with all the passion of a true love," to use Benedict XVI's words. And that means "his love may certainly be called *eros*"—an eros so pure "as to become one with *agape*."[15] To this day, in preparation for Holy Communion, the Eastern Church prays with words first written by Saint John Chrysostom in the fourth century: "You have smitten me with yearning, O Christ, and by your divine eros you have changed me . . . grant me to be filled with delight in you . . . leaping for joy."[16] Divine eros changes us by orienting human eros toward that which truly satisfies, giving us hope and filling us with delight. This is the Eucharist: where human eros leaps for joy in discovering divine eros. Indeed, our yearning for God is but a dim reflection of his yearning for us.

Furthermore, since grace perfects nature, just as it is in an ordinary meal, so it is in the Eucharist: that which we

---

14 Saint Hilary of Poitiers, *The Trinity*, 1, 1–13, as cited in Olivier Clement, *The Roots of Christian Mysticism*, 21.
15 Benedict XVI, *Deus Caritas Est* 9, 10.
16 *The Divine Liturgy of Our Father among the Saints John Chrysostom*, Pew Edition (Greek Orthodox Archdiocese of America, 2018), 79.

eat must die so that we might live. But here, in a dramatic reversal of hunter and hunted, the hungry ones don't have to track and kill their food. The "Hound of Heaven," as Francis Thompson[17] famously described the Lord, is on the hunt for us—not to *eat* us, but to *feed* us! This hunter freely dies so *we* (the hunted) can live: "No one takes my life from me; I lay it down on my own" (Jn 10:18); "This is my body, which is given for you. . . . This cup is my blood, which is shed for you" (Lk 22:19). The logic of the food chain tells us that the weaker one is *always* fodder for the mightier one. But here the Almighty One assures us: "I'm not here to *eat* you; I'm here to *feed* you. Open your yearning to me and I will offer you my very self, satisfying your hunger with the finest wheat, slaking your thirst with the most intoxicating wine."[18]

What might an appropriate response be to so great a gift? I'd suggest, as I did above in reference to an ordinary meal, that we should begin by giving thanks for the life that was sacrificed. That's what the Church's liturgy is, for that is what the word "eucharist" means: *thanksgiving*. Those who are in touch with their hunger for a life-not-bound-by-death and discover the promise of the Eucharist offered in the Church's liturgy—"Whoever eats my flesh and drinks my blood has eternal life, and I will raise him on the last day" (Jn 6:54)—cannot help but live a life of hope and joy and thanksgiving.

---

17 Francis Thompson (1859–1907) was an English poet and Catholic mystic who lived for a time in extreme poverty, essentially homeless and addicted to opium, until a prostitute found him in his destitution and offered him lodging (he would later describe her in his poetry as his "savior"). He had also contemplated suicide in his despair, but saw a vision that gave him hope.

18 There is a sense, as we will touch on in Chapter 6, in which God also "feeds" on us. He is hungry and thirsty for us to be hungry and thirsty for him. Beside Jacob's well, Christ first asks us for a drink (see CCC 2560).

By dying and rising, Christ has passed over to the Life where "death no longer has power over him" (Rom 6:9), to the Life he had with the Father before time began (see Jn 17:5). The difference now is that, having wed himself forever to human nature in the womb of Mary, the second Person of the Trinity participates *bodily* in the ecstasy and bliss of the eternal exchange of Love. *This* is the promise of the Eucharist; this is the theophany to be discovered in the visceralness of hunger and thirst and bread and wine and digestive juices: we, too, are destined by God the Father to participate *bodily* with Christ in the eternal exchange of Love, where his joy will be *in* us, our joy will be complete (see Jn 15:11), and no one will take our joy from us (see Jn 16:22).

The Life That Is Totally Fulfilling

"The Bible calls that secure life, *eternal* life," says Albacete. "You see, eternal life doesn't mean, in the Bible, simply that it lasts forever. It's not just that. . . . No, it's that it's fulfilling *totally*. Every moment. And its *most* fulfilling characteristic is that it is secure, that it is strong—that *you don't have to eat it like a bird!* That it actually will sustain you, that it will destroy the forces of death and chaos. Eternal life—that is what we are looking for!"[19]

Albacete thus proposes a firm answer to Christ's all-important question ("What are you looking for?"). The path that leads to the fulfillment of our deepest desires begins by getting in touch with those desires. We must give ourselves permission to *feel* the tremors of that sacred eros that throbs at the core of our humanity, without shutting it down *and*

---

19 Lorenzo Albacete, *Retrieve* video series, episode 2.

without aiming it at bogus satisfactions. That's easier said than done, of course, but there's really no alternative. And we can trust that having the courage to *feel* the ache will itself jostle us toward the true object of our longing. As C.S. Lewis says, "I knew only too well how easily the longing accepts false objects and through what dark ways the pursuit of them leads us. But I also saw that the Desire itself contains the corrective of all these errors."[20]

Desire itself. If heaven is a wedding feast (Rev 19:9), then it's our deepest hunger that will point us in the right direction. "Show me one who is full of longing, one who is hungry," says Saint Augustine, "and he knows what I mean. But if I speak to someone without feeling, he does not understand what I am saying." Then, taking on the voice of Christ, Augustine says: "I give each what he loves, I give each the object of his hope. . . . What he now hungers for, he will eat; what he now thirsts for, he will drink to the full. When? At the resurrection of the dead, for *I will raise him up on the last day.*"[21]

Everything about the Christian faith hinges on the bodily death and Resurrection of Christ, and on the hope that, because Christ died and rose, we who are baptized into Christ will also rise from the dead to eternal life. Indeed, if Christ was not raised from the dead, our faith is in vain (see 1 Cor 15:17). But if Christ's body *was* raised from the dead, then "the saying which seems to be only a beautiful dream is in fact true: 'Love is strong as death.'"[22] In fact, it is *stronger.*

---

20 C.S. Lewis, *The Pilgrim's Regress* (Eerdmans Publishing Co., 2014), 237.

21 Taken from the Office of Readings, Thursday of the 28th Week in Ordinary Time; treatise on John by Saint Augustine, Tract. 26, 4–6: CCL 36, 261–63.

22 Ratzinger, *Introduction to Christianity*, 230.

INTO THE MYSTIC

1. What's something you learned in this chapter that you hadn't known before?

2. How have you experienced in your own life "the basic problem of human existence"? In other words, when and how have you experienced the cry of your heart for something more than what this world provides?

3. Have you ever reflected on the profundity and sacredness of eating? Have you ever pondered the connection between digestion and divinization (in Jesus divinizing whatever he ate, and in us being divinized by eating the Eucharist)? How can you help yourself and those you love to enter into the sacredness of an ordinary meal as a reminder of the extraordinary meal of the Eucharist?

4. Do you believe that love is stronger than death? What difference does that make in your day-to-day life?

CHAPTER 3

The Scandal of Beauty's Revelation

**Absolute, impeccable beauty . . .
appeared in the flesh.**

—KAROL WOJTYLA[1]

It was decades ago, but I remember it as though it were this morning. Monsignor Albacete came into the classroom, sat in his chair, lit up a cigarette (a regular occurrence in a building plastered with No Smoking signs), and as if he were trying to convey an encounter he had had with Absolute Beauty itself, uttered in his Puerto Rican accent, "The

---

1   Karol Wojtyla, *God Is Beauty: A Retreat on the Gospel and Art* (TOB Institute Press, 2021), 25.

scandal of the *hic*." After a long drag on his brightly ashing Marlboro, he paused long enough it seemed for the nicotine to hit his blood, then said again on his smoke-wafting exhale, "The scaaaaandaaaal . . . of the *HIC!*"

Since English wasn't his first language, despite the sense of awe he conveyed, I honestly thought he might be mispronouncing "hickey" and wondered if we were in for a lecture on the perils of making out. He then explained that in the Basilica of the Annunciation in Nazareth, on the altar that marks the place believed to be where Mary gave her consent, we read the familiar words of John's Gospel: *Verbum caro factum est*—the Word was made flesh. "But in that place," he said with amazement, "there is one little word added to it that's different: *hic*, 'here'—*Verbum caro hic factum est.* . . . The Word was made flesh *here*."

Turns out, he was indeed trying to convey something of an encounter he had had with Absolute Beauty itself. And he was inviting us to encounter it with him. It is a Beauty, a Mystery that he insisted again and again was not abstract, it was not an intellectual idea or concept, it was not "out there" somewhere. The Mystery, Transcendent Beauty itself, he insisted, had been made manifest. The *Logos*—the Logic, Meaning, Purpose, Design, Destiny, Goodness, and Reason in which everything lives and moves and has its being (see Acts 17:28)—*that* Mystery, he insisted, had become concrete in a specific place at a specific time; it had become visible, tangible, something one could encounter and experience with the senses. As one of John Paul II's poems expresses it:

You seek out people everywhere.
But to seek everywhere, you had to stop in some place.

You chose this.

The whole earth comes to this one land.[2]

That is the scandal of the *hic* and *that* is the scandal of the Christian proposal. It's one thing to believe God is the Almighty Creator who dwells outside, above, and beyond the universe he created. It's another thing altogether to affirm that that same God has entered the universe he created and dwells right *hic*. It's the scandal of the *Omnipresent* making himself *particularly present*, of the One who is present everywhere being acutely, tangibly present right *here*. And how here? What enables the *here*? What the heck justifies the *hic*?

The Body Is the Very Soul of Christianity

The Bible places these words in the eternal heart of the second Person of the Trinity: "A body you have prepared for me" (Heb 10:5). That brief sentence, in fact, "contains the entire Gospel" and "the whole fullness of Sacred Scripture," Cardinal Ratzinger maintains.[3] If the Incarnation is real, it means that Ultimate Beauty has been manifested in human flesh. (Ah! You see, there's a good reason we are attracted to the human body!) If the Incarnation is real, we encounter God not by fleeing the physical world, but by entering its inmost depths. The Lord "comes not from above, but from within, so that we might find him in this world of ours."[4] We must say it again: it happened in a specific time and in a specific place. It's not an abstraction. If we miss the time-and-space bodily concreteness of Christ, we miss the Gospel message *entirely*,

---

2   John Paul II, *The Place Within* (Random House, 1982), 112.

3   Ratzinger, *Mary: The Church at the Source*, 91.

4   Pope Francis, *Laudato Si* 236.

Albacete used to emphasize. The sensualness of it all—the fact that Absolute Beauty reveals itself in and through the "schtuff" of the material world—couldn't be more crucial.

G.K. Chesterton observes that a "mystical materialism marked Christianity from its birth; the very soul of it was a body."[5] What a remarkable turn of phrase! Although Chesterton is expressing a truth as ancient as the Incarnation itself, it's not typically the way people conceive of biblical faith, not even those who claim to profess it. Today, a great many Christians have been "evangelized" by the culture at large and thus live as functional Gnostics. This ancient dualistic heresy involves a death-dealing rupture of body and soul, positing human identity in spirit (thought-will-intellect) and salvation in the soul's deliverance from the "crudeness" of matter through a secret knowledge offering spiritual enlightenment (*gnosis* means "knowledge"). It's death dealing because death, by definition, is the rupture of body and soul, and all the dualistic heresies take that rupture as their foundational principle.[6]

Today's rampant Gnostic split is largely the result of the fact that Western culture has been steeping itself in Rene Descartes's dictum "I think, therefore, I am" for nearly four

---

5   G.K. Chesterton, *A Short History of England* (John Lane Company, 1917), 36.
6   The following story is recounted by Father Peter John Cameron in his endorsement of Albacete's posthumous book *The Relevance of the Stars* (Slant, 2021). While attending a Catholic rally in New York City, two bystanders approached Albacete and asked, "Is this a protest?" He spontaneously and exuberantly replied, "Yes!" They asked, "What are you protesting?" "*Dualism!*" he exclaimed. As the perplexed inquisitors turned to walk away, Albacete shouted after them, "Don't go! The dualists will get you!" Beyond illustrating Albacete's inimitable genius and quick wit, this story reveals his deeply held conviction that the Catholic Church exists precisely to hold together in integral unity what the rest of the world seems hell-bent on tearing apart.

centuries. Imbibing this Cartesian brew has brought about a new "common sense" that considers the human person to be a "thinking thing" housed in meaningless matter. Despite all the culture's emphasis on "identity," we are being sold a vision of ourselves as no-bodies—quite literally. The Church, to the contrary, has always proclaimed and vigorously defended the truth that the human person is not no-body, nor is he just any-body; the human person is *some*-body. The Church has paid a high price for defending the truth that human identity is rooted in the marriage of flesh and spirit. Nonetheless, the modern world has had its way with the vast majority of Christians, and today, as the Eastern Orthodox theologian Timothy Patitsas put it, "we have a disembodied faith for a disembodied people."[7]

The proof of this disembodiment of the Christian faith (a gross contradiction in terms, as we will come to see) is to be found in the widespread rebellion *by those within the Church* against the Church's teaching on matters of sexuality, gender, and marriage. We will return to this in subsequent chapters. First, however, for that rebellion to be put in context, we need to spend some time getting reacquainting with our embodied selves and with the logic of the Incarnation.

Salvation *of* the Flesh, Not *from* the Flesh

Saint Thomas Aquinas describes the human person as the horizon of creation, the place where the land and the sky meet.[8] Created from the dust of the earth and the very breath

---

7   Timothy Patitsas, "Chastity and Empathy: Eros, Agape, and the Mystery of the Twofold Anointing," *Road to Emmaus Journal* (Winter 2015), 23.
8   See Prologue to the Third Book of Thomas Aquinas's *Commentary on the Sentences of Peter Lombard*.

of God (see Gen 2:7), we are a strange marriage of humus and heaven, dirt and deity, spit and spirit. We are embodied souls, spiritualized bodies. The soul is not an "immaterial self" housed in a nonspiritual body. Rather, the human soul is what makes the human body what it is: not just *a* body, but *some*-body. We're not persons "in" a body as the Cartesian view would have us believe; we're *body-persons*. This means the body is not something we "have" or "own"; the living body is the living person. What we do with our bodies, we do with ourselves, just as what is done to our bodies is done to ourselves.

Saint John Paul II puts it succinctly when he asserts that the "body expresses the person. It is, thus, in all its materiality . . . penetrable and transparent, as it were, in such a way as to make it clear who man is (and who he ought to be)."[9] Here we are back to the concept of sacramentality: the physical reality of the human person (the body) is a sign that makes visible the spiritual truth of the human person (the soul). "The body, in fact, and only the body," says John Paul II, "is capable of making visible what is invisible."[10] In this sense the body is the sacrament of the invisible mystery of the soul.

"The unity of soul and body is so profound," says the *Catechism*, "that one has to consider the soul to be the 'form' of the body."[11] We can recognize the truth of this statement in the fact that, when the soul separates from the body at death, the body de-forms. If we are inclined to think of death as the moment of the soul's "liberation" from the body, we need to be reminded that this is the teaching of Plato, not of Scripture, which boldly proclaims faith in the resurrection of our bodies.

9   John Paul II, TOB 7:2.
10   John Paul II, TOB 19:4.
11   CCC 365.

This means that the truth about man's destiny "cannot be understood as a state of the soul alone, separated (according to Plato, liberated) from the body, but must be understood as *the definitively and perfectly 'integrated' state of man* brought about by a [perfect] union of the soul with the body."[12]

Saint Paul's admonitions to live by "the Spirit" and not by "the flesh" (see Gal 5:16–17; Rom 8:4–8) do not condone a rupture of matter and spirit. In his terminology, to live by "the flesh" means to be cut off *in both body and soul* from God's in-spiration (God's breathing-into). In turn, those who open themselves authentically to life "according to the Spirit" do *not* reject their bodies; their bodies become the very temple of the Spirit (see 1 Cor 6:19–20). In this way, life in the Spirit becomes at one and the same time "the redemption of our bodies" (Rom 8:23). Cardinal Cantalamessa recalls that the "Fathers of the Church, in combating the Gnostics, used to say the Gospel does not proclaim salvation *from* the flesh but salvation *of* the flesh."[13] Christ is "the savior of the body" (Eph 5:23). *Our* bodies are saved by *his* body which, given up for us in the Eucharist, is the source and summit of the Christian faith. It is here, in the liturgical and sacramental life of the Church, says renowned liturgist and theologian Alexander Schmemann, that the "opposition of the 'spiritual' and the 'material' . . . is denounced, abolished, and revealed as a monstrous lie about God and man and the world."[14]

An authentically Christian spirituality is *always* incarnational. It's always a *"spirituality of the body."*[15] If I want a

---

12 John Paul II, TOB 66:6.
13 Raniero Cantalamessa, Address of March 23, 2018.
14 Alexander Schmemann, *For the Life of the World* (Saint Vladimir's Seminary Press, 1973), 76.
15 John Paul II, TOB 59:4.

spiritual path that does not involve my body and Christ's body, and the whole physical world, then my spirituality is no longer Christian. It's Gnostic.[16] Contrary to popular belief, "spiritual" does not mean some excarnate, otherworldly reality. "Spiritual designates a human reality, a human experience—namely, the experience of limitless desire," as Monsignor Albacete puts it. The spiritual life designates the experience of the "human orientation to infinity."[17] And precisely because the Infinite One has wed himself to this physical world, "the spiritual sphere is discovered only by deeper involvement with the corporeal sphere," as Father Jose Granados affirms. "To say that an experience is spiritual means that it inserts us more deeply among [physical] things and events so as to disclose the transcendence they contain. . . . For this reason we must say: the more spiritual an experience is, the more it leads us to live the body fully."[18]

Living the body fully means recognizing matter as "the proper form of love."[19] The entire material world is summed up in the human body and comes to fulfillment inasmuch as love is revealed through the human body.[20] In this fallen world, however, matter resists the incarnation of love. We rebel against love's bodily demands, often violently. This is the treacherous milieu in which the *Logos* weds himself to human flesh, suffering that violence fully *in his flesh*, absorbing it in love. Precisely by doing so, the *Logos* fulfills matter,

---

16 See Patitsas, "Chastity and Empathy," 22.
17 Lorenzo Albacete, *The Relevance of the Stars: Christ, Culture, and Destiny*, 128.
18 Jose Granados, "Theology of the Body as Necessary to Understanding Life in the Spirit," *Communio* (Summer 2016), 191–92.
19 See Grygiel, *Discovering the Human Person in Conversation with John Paul II*, 50.
20 See CCC 364.

once and for all, as the proper form of love. Of course, this doesn't automatically quell our rebellion nor lead to a global embrace of Jesus Christ as God-in-the-flesh. Indeed, a culture intent on divorcing itself from the body can make *zero sense* of a God who is intent on wedding himself to it.

The following sentiment, voiced by an appalled Muslim, expresses well the outrageousness of the Christian proposal: "Imagine believing that a woman gave birth to God, The Most-High, and that he needed to be breastfed and taken care of by his own creation. Imagine believing that God used to defecate and urinate upon himself and had to be cleaned by his mother. Exalted is Allah! Above their lies!"[21] He's right: Christmas faith proclaims that God's realm is not limited to that of the spirit—he has willed to penetrate *matter*, making her *mater* (mother) . . . of God! God-sucking-at-the breast, God-in-diapers *is* a scandal—at least to those who take offense at the body and its functions, thinking them irredeemably beneath the holiness of God. But where does this idea of the body's "unholiness" come from? Could there be an enemy who has convinced us that our bodies are "offensive" precisely to block us from "every spiritual blessing in the heavens" that God wants to bestow on us through *the body* of Christ (see Eph 1:3)? Christ himself asserts: "Blessed is he who takes no offense at me" (Mt 11:6).

Clothing the Body with Incorruptibility

Spiritually minded people of various religious backgrounds often have a tendency to fly away from that which is bodily.

---

21 This was posted by a Muslim on Twitter amid the Christmas preparations of Advent 2019.

The fact that the body is bound by death is deeply embedded in our psyche. Hence, we are led to believe that to reach the lasting and eternal we must leave the body behind and transcend the physical world. As we've been unfolding, this desire for the Transcendent, for the Mystery, for the Beauty, for the *Logos* behind it all is what makes us human. But does reaching the Transcendent demand that we leave the physical behind?

We've seen that the cry of the heart (eros) puts us all on an inherently religious quest. Here it's illuminating that the word "religion" has origins in the Latin *religare*, meaning "to form a bond." From this perspective we can affirm with Cardinal Cantalamessa that "human sexuality is the first school of religion."[22] Stamped right in our bodies—right in the sexual difference itself—is the religious call to form bonds. If such is the case, why then is religion so often thought to demand a flight from the body to reach God? Christianity presents us with the exact opposite movement: God taking on a body to reach us! If all that matters is the "spirit," we would have to wonder "why God did not choose a simpler path and present himself as spirit to man's spirit so as to impart his grace to him?" asks Ratzinger. Man's relationship to God, he continues, "if it is to be a human relationship to God, must be just as man is: corporeal."[23]

To the degree that we let the indispensableness of our bodies sink in, it radically changes our very concept of living a "spiritual" life. We discover, as Father Granados observes, that someone "who wants to realize the openness of the human spirit toward the divine does not need to elevate [his

---

22 Raniero Cantalamessa, Fourth Lenten Homily, 2016.

23 Joseph Ratzinger, *Collected Works: Theology of the Liturgy* (Ignatius Press, 2014), 166.

spirit]; instead he must, so to speak, humiliate it, bring it closer to the humus of the flesh, so as thus to open it from within to something greater. In reality, the concept of spirit as something opposed to matter," he concludes, "is foreign to Scripture."[24]

What, then, are we to make of biblical statements like this: "the corruptible body burdens the soul" (Wis 9:15)? I know that burden well. I'm getting old. I'm going gray. I have age spots and wrinkles on my face that, not so long ago, weren't there. My joints are getting creaky and I can't do nearly as many push-ups as I once could. These are all signs that I'm returning to dust. Not a comforting realization, to say the least. When I'm not distracted by my go-to numbing agents, I experience a soul-shaking, bone-rattling cry to be saved from this burden, to be saved from death. But to pursue a resolution that involves eschewing my body doesn't do justice to the truth of my humanity. In a poem called *Thoughts on Maturing*, John Paul II wrote that maturity is "a descent to a hidden core" where "the surface meets the depth" and the soul is "more reconciled with the body." That very reconciliation, however, makes us "more opposed to death" and "uneasy about the resurrection." Is it real? Can I link my future—my *eternal* destiny—with my body? The human person is no longer himself "if he cannot link his future with his body."[25]

This uneasiness about the relationship of our bodies to our future confronts us with *the* struggle of human life. Angelistic Platonism (my soul will be liberated from my body

24 Jose Granados, "Theology of the Body as Necessary to Understanding Life in the Spirit," *Communio* (Summer 2016), 177.
25 John Paul II, *The Place Within*, 153, 154.

at death) and nihilistic materialism (when I die, all that's left of me is a rotting corpse) present opposite loopholes to avoid that struggle. I must wrestle with the One who took flesh and declared: "I AM the resurrection" (Jn 11:25). The *descent* into flesh of God's eternal Son and the *ascent* of his flesh into the eternal realm teach us that our desire to fly away from that which ties us down will be fulfilled not by ridding ourselves of the flesh, but by *trustingly accepting its demise as the path to its eventual transfiguration*. If Christ *is* the resurrection, then those who die in him can do so in confidence that the "sepulcher becomes a birth canal," as David Fagerberg confidently expresses it.[26] Indeed, the Gospel offers the hope and promise that, through a new kind of birth, Christ "will change our lowly body to conform to his glorified body" (Phil 3:21).

This is what Peter, James, and John glimpsed on Mount Tabor when Christ's body was transfigured before them: "While he was praying his face changed in appearance and his clothing became dazzling white" (Lk 9:29). Saint Andrew of Crete observes that "the impossible beauty" radiating from Christ's "spotless flesh" was too much for the apostles to endure. "For if his garments are such because of the brilliance that gushes forth from within, what must the glory be that is wrapped and hidden by these garments . . . ?"[27] And, as the Preface of the Mass has it on the feast of the Transfiguration, Christ revealed "the greatest splendor of that bodily form which he shares with all humanity . . . that he might show

---

26 David Fagerberg, *Liturgical Mysticism* (Emmaus Academic, 2019), 11.

27 Saint Andrew of Crete, "On the Transfiguration of Christ the Lord" (Sermon 7), published in *Light on the Mountain: Greek Patristic and Byzantine Homilies on the Transfiguration of the Lord,* Brian E. Daley (Saint Vladimir's Seminary Press, 2013).

how in the Body of the whole Church is to be fulfilled what so wonderfully shown forth first in its Head." As Christ goes, so go those who follow him. Saint Paul sums up our hope in Christ when he says "that which is corruptible will clothe itself with incorruptibility" (1 Cor 15:53).

We are rightly reminded at the start of Lent that we are dust and to dust we shall return. But let us never forget that in and through Christ we are not merely dust destined for death; we are also dust destined through death for divinization! Recognizing humanity's powerlessness in the face of death, John Paul II proclaims, "You God, you alone can retrieve our bodies from the earth."[28] And he has promised us that he will (see Jn 6:40). This means that our bodiliness is not an obstacle to the Transcendence for which we yearn. In fact, it's made for it! Destined for it! Meant for it! The body is meant for the Lord, as Saint Paul tells us. Then, even more astonishingly, he asserts that the Lord is meant for the body (see 1 Cor 6:13). Commenting on this passage, John Paul II says: "It is difficult to express more concisely what the mystery of the Incarnation implies for every believer."[29] Unfortunately, this is one of those verses that typically goes in one ear and out the other. If we were to enter into it, it would dramatically rearrange how we perceive the entire universe and our place within it.

The Body Is Meant for the Lord

There is no experience of any reality for human beings that does not reach us through our bodies. Our bodies are at the

28 John Paul II, *The Place Within*, 159.
29 John Paul II, TOB 56:4.

very origin of all our relationships to reality. So, if I have the capacity as a human being to discover meaning in the realities I experience (what we've called "the divine sense of humor," "sacramentality," and "theophany"), *the very first* of these is the meaning of the body. Experientially, I may recognize the beauty of the rest of creation before I am able to recognize the beauty of my own body, but the meaning of my body is not just one more experience to understand among many. It is the *fundamental* one. From the meaning of the body, everything else follows. When we live and experience the true *meaning of our bodies*, we flourish. When we fail to do so, we flounder.[30]

The body is *meant* for the Lord. That's its meaning. But what does *that* mean? Benedict XVI tells us that the second verse of Psalm 63 takes us to the heart of the matter: "O God, you are my God—it is you I seek! For you my body yearns; for you my soul thirsts, like a dry land without water." Here the cry of eros reveals that not "only my soul, but even every fiber of my flesh is made to find its peace, its fulfillment in God."[31] My body (*not just my soul!*) has a Transcendent destiny and God-given orientation toward the Infinite.

Why, then, are we so prone to think that a "Godly life" necessitates the negation of the body? Recall that Christ is "the savior of the body" (Eph 5:23). He came bodily so that we might experience "the redemption of our bodies" (Rom 8:23). This implies that something has gone wrong with the

---

30 Thoughts here are adapted from an unpublished lecture by Lorenzo Albacete on the Theology of the Body given at the University of San Francisco in 1995.

31 Benedict XVI, Letter addressing the *Communion and Liberation* gathering in Rimini, Italy, August 10, 2012.

way we experience our own bodiliness in this fallen world. Indeed, since the dawn of sin, the body's God-given Transcendent orientation must now reckon with the inescapable pull of the grave. The inner conflict we feel between our aspiration for the stars and the fact that our bodies will be eaten by worms instills in us a deep uneasiness with our embodied selves. The inevitability of death, not to mention all manner of bodily sufferings along the way, can lead us to resent, reject, and even disdain bodiliness. It can lead us to *prefer* that Gnostic, disembodied version of the "self" as a means of self-preservation.

But where did death come from? It didn't come from God. "For God formed us to be imperishable; the image of his own nature he made us. But by the envy of the devil, death entered the world" (Wis 2:23–24). Lucifer, let us recall, was created by God as an angel of light (that's what "lucifer" means). What do we have that angels don't have? Bodies. And *our bodies are meant for the Lord.* In fact, by virtue of the stunning wonder of the Incarnation, the human body is destined to be raised *higher than the angels* to participate in the eternal intoxicating bliss of the Trinity in a way that angels cannot experience. This is what Lucifer, and all the angels who fell with him, came to envy. Father Francesco Bamonte, an experienced exorcist, writes that, upon creating the angels,

> God would have, in some way, shown to all the angels the future image of the Son, God made man, Christ Jesus, inviting them to recognize in him, from that point on, their head and Lord. Lucifer and one part of the angels refused to adore a man inferior to them by nature. . . . The divine project of the Incarnation is considered by them to be an

unheard-of offense to their own angelic dignity and to their own greatness in the hierarchy of beings. Therefore, they rejected it with indignation. . . . Lucifer expected that the . . . union of the Word [with his creatures] would take place not with human nature but necessarily and exclusively with his angelic nature. [Hence] the sin of Lucifer was envy . . . [and] Lucifer subsequently deceived man because of envy.[32]

Envy is deeper than jealousy. Jealousy says, "I wish I had what you had." But envy goes further and says, "I hate that you have it; I wish that you didn't have it; and I want you to hate that you have it as much as I do." The fallen angels *hate* our bodies with all their demonic rage and fury, and they are literally hell-bent on getting us to hate them as well. With some trepidation we can learn what God values from what demons despise: "The repugnance that we experienced when he entered into that flesh, only we know!" screeched a demon during an exorcism Father Bamonte was performing. "I am pure spirit. Why not I instead of that nature? . . . He incarnates himself in your disgusting body made of worms. Why did he do it? To ruin us? . . . I cannot bear this. That putrid flesh!"[33]

The enemy's repugnance toward the human body is writ large in our world today. The spiritual battle is *raging*, and the battlefield is the body. The two sides are clear: the elites of the world insist that our bodies are *meaningless*; the Church insists that our bodies reveal *ultimate Meaning*. Christianity proposes to the world that ultimate Meaning itself—the *Logos*—took

32 Francesco Bamonte, *The Virgin Mary and the Devil in Exorcisms*, 2nd English Edition (Pope Leo XIII Institute, 2010), 57–58.
33 Ibid., 60–62.

flesh. But the Incarnation is not just the embodiment of ultimate Meaning; it is also the ultimate en-meaning-ment of the body. For those with eyes to see, our bodies tell the ultimate story; they reveal the mystery hidden for all eternity in God (more on this in the next chapter).

The body is *meant* for the Lord and the Lord is *meant* for the body! Evangelization is *this* proclamation in all its fullness, in all its splendor, and in all its astonishingly wondrous implications. Indeed, since the body is the very soul of Christianity, "when evangelization is lacking in a person or in a culture, the barometer where its lack is most clearly seen is the attitude toward the body, the attitude toward the physical," says Albacete. "Indeed," he continues, "it is the desperate confusion and disarray with respect to human bodiliness, as shown in human sexuality, that shows the need for evangelization."[34]

This absolutely inseparable relation between the Gospel and the experience of the body can be seen in the fact that from the very beginning the *greatest* enemy of Christianity has been the attempt to separate Christ from the flesh. How can I distinguish a good spirit and a bad spirit? It's very simple: everything that affirms Christ-in-the-flesh is of God, Saint John tells us; everything that ruptures Christ from the flesh comes from the antichrist (see 1 Jn 4:1–3). Everything that detaches the Gospel from the physical becomes an abstraction, an idealism. And it is not only un-Christian, it is *anti*-Christian. It is attempting to destroy Christianity, removing both its scandal and its potency by reducing it to all kinds of abstract intellectual proposals.[35]

---

34 Lorenzo Albacete, unpublished lecture on the Theology of the Body.
35 Ideas and phrases expressed in this paragraph taken from ibid.

The Lord Is Meant for the Body

The *Catechism* observes that "from the beginning, God envisaged the glory of the new creation in Christ" and states that the Incarnation and Resurrection are "in accordance with God's eternal plan."[36] If the Lord is *meant* for the body (and the body is *meant* for the Lord), then the Incarnation is not "plan B." What happened in "the fullness of time" (Gal 4:4) was integral to the divine plan for creation "before time began" (2 Tim 1:9). This means that Christ did not come in the flesh only because we sinned. He suffered and died in the flesh because we sinned, but sin does not have the power to thwart God's eternal plan for creation. "The plan of the Lord stands forever" (Ps 33:11). Sin, we might say, took that plan on a tragic detour. The forgiveness of sins is now the prerequisite for restoring us to the plan the Father had established in Christ "before the foundation of the world" (Eph 1:4).

From the very beginning, all things were created *for* Christ, Saint Paul tells us (see Col 1:16). God the Father created the universe as a gift for his eternal Son. He designed it precisely in such a way that his divine Son could be at home within it; so that he who is eternal and invisible could dwell within the temporal and visible and wed himself to it. Why would he want to do that? Dionysius the Areopagite says, "we must dare to affirm (for this is the truth)" that the eternal Son was "transported outside of himself" toward creatures "through his excessive erotic goodness . . . and ecstatic power" (the Greek *ekstasis* means "to go outside oneself"). For those who open to this power, "the divine *eros* also brings ecstasy, not allowing those who are touched by it to belong

---

36 CCC 280 and 653; see also John Paul II, TOB 96:2–5.

to themselves, but only to the beloved. . . . And hence the great Paul, compelled by the divine *eros*, and having received a share in its ecstatic power, says, with inspired utterance, 'I live, and yet no longer I, but Christ lives in me.' These are the words of a true *erotic* and ecstatic toward God."[37]

The point is that divine Love is diffusive of itself. It's outrageous in its gen-*eros*-ity.[38] It wants others to know its own joy, to participate in its own bliss. God wants to wed himself to creation so that what is *not-God* could be divinized; so that what is *not-God* could be taken up into the Life that *is-God*, taken up into the glory that the Son enjoyed before time began in the eternal exchange of Life-giving Love.[39]

The three Persons of the Trinity are totally at home in each other because each is divine. But what in the created order has the capacity to participate in the divine bliss? What reality that is *not-God* has the capacity of allowing that which *is-God* to be so intimately "at home" in its non-God-ness that what *is-God* can BECOME what is *not-God* without losing anything of himself that *is-God*? Whatever it is, it must be "little less than a god" itself (Ps 8:6). It must be the absolute pinnacle of all of visible creation's beauty and goodness. It must be the gathering up of all the wonder and elegance of all of the earth's creatures, of all the oceans' secrets, of all the mysteries contained in the mind-boggling expanse of the heavens (and the galaxies, stars, planets, and moons contained therein). Whatever it is, it must be the high point

---

37 Dionysius the Areopagite, *The Divine Names*, 4.13.

38 While the word "eros" is not actually part of the etymology of the word "generosity," it is a happy coincidence to find "eros" at the center of this word.

39 See Lorenzo Albacete, *Retrieve* video series, episode 6.

of the divine sense of humor—what makes God laugh (and when something this sacred is desecrated, weep) the most. It must be the high point of sacramentality and theophany—far more compelling in its wooing to everlasting Beauty than all the pinkish-purplish petals of all the redbud trees that have ever existed.

Where do we find it?

Look no further than the mirror. Your body-person tells *this* story: the story that God wants to wed himself to his creation so that what is *not-God* could be made God.[40] Yes, God took on flesh so that your flesh and mine could take on God, making us "partakers of the divine nature" (2 Pt 1:4). God was *humanized* so man could be *divinized*! This is none other than to say: the Lord is meant for the body and the body is meant for the Lord.

We can be tempted right here to balk in disbelief. But let us take stock of Christmas. If we believe in the Christmas story—not just as some vague invitation to "peace on earth," but as the story of God himself taking on flesh and being born of a woman (see Gal 4:4)—then this is what we believe about *our own* bodies as male and female: they tell the story of Christmas; they tell the story of the marriage of heaven and earth; they tell the story that God was *humanized* so we humans could be *divinized*. If the Mystery behind it all really

---

40 The *Catechism* quotes Saint Athanasius: "For the Son of God became man so that we might become God" (460). Obviously this cannot be taken to mean a self-appropriation of the divine life. Such self-appropriation is the very essence of the original sin: "You will be like God . . ." (Gen 3:5). Man is not the absolute. However, he is invited by the Absolute to open his heart to the greatest gift that the Creator could possibly bestow upon a creature: man is invited to be *"partner of the Absolute"* (John Paul II, TOB 6:2).

and truly took flesh to reveal in our flesh the Mystery behind it all, then that's what our bodies are *meant* to do: reveal the ultimate Mystery. If Christmas is real, then *your body* is meant for the Lord, and the Lord is meant for *your body*.

Our first parents already knew *something* of this mystery in the beginning. Since their innocence (prior to sin) was an experience of grace, "we must deduce that *the reality of the creation of man* was already *permeated* by the perennial election of man in Christ," says John Paul II. "From the 'beginning,' man, male and female, shared in this supernatural gift. This endowment was given in view of [Christ] . . . although—according to the dimensions of time and history—it preceded the Incarnation." The grace of original innocence, therefore, "was brought about precisely *out of regard for [Christ]* . . . while chronologically anticipating his coming in the body."[41] Tragically, our first parents forfeited this original grace by breaking the covenant, and access to the tree of Life (to divinization in its fullness) was denied them. Christ's coming in the flesh, once again, was not *only* for the sake of forgiving that betrayal, but abounded even more in establishing a New Covenant in his flesh "between God and humanity [that] opens an infinite perspective of Life: and access to the Tree of Life—according to the original plan of the God of the covenant—is revealed to every man in its definitive fullness. This will be the meaning of Christ's death and resurrection; this will be the testimony of the paschal mystery," says John Paul II.[42] The eternal plan of God the Father has been fulfilled *in the flesh of his Son*.

41 John Paul II, TOB 96:4–5.
42 Ibid., 65:6.

The Symbolic and the Diabolic

As we said earlier in this chapter, today, a great many Christians, having been "evangelized" by the culture at large, live as functional Gnostics. When the actual implications of God-in-the-flesh are unfolded, we resist. Sometimes we even revolt. "Religion is a *spiritual* thing," people insist. "The body is a carnal thing and 'carnal things' are of the devil!" we've heard. Oh, how the deceiver loves to take partial truths and turn them into lies that destroy us! God is pure Spirit, there's no doubt about that. But in the fullness of time that same God became flesh, which means that in Christ, Spirit and matter "are of one accord" (1 Jn 5:8). If "carnal things" are "of the devil," then the In-*carn*-ation is blasphemous.

Don't you see? The devil is after our bodies! Whether he gets them through tempting us to bodily revelry or bodily revulsion, it makes no difference to him. Either way, he's robbed us of the very soul of Christianity!

The deceiver appears as an angel of light to get good-hearted people who want to do the *right* thing to move in the *wrong* direction. If we want to be in step with the Holy Spirit, the direction in which he always moves is *incarnation*: the marriage, the unity, the bringing together of flesh and spirit, so that spiritual and divine mysteries can become tangible, visible, sacramental. The direction in which the evil spirit always moves is *excarnation*: the divorce, the rupture, the splitting apart of flesh and spirit, so that spiritual and divine mysteries remain intangible, invisible, and inaccessible.

Incarnation versus excarnation: this is the battle! The consecration (making holy/sacred) of the physical versus the desecration (making unholy) of the physical: this is the war between the Word and the anti-Word, the Church and the anti-Church, between good and evil, life and death, love and all that is opposed to love. We're all engaged in this cosmic struggle whether we realize it or not. And because the body is the very soul of Christianity, the body is at the heart and center of the battle. Our daily choices, attitudes, behaviors, and actions, all of which manifest themselves in our bodies, tilt us in one direction or the other. There's no neutral ground. As Nicholas Healy observes, "The use that we make of our bodies is either a true confession of Christ or a counter witness to him; it is either Catholic or heretical."[43]

But until we realize the nature of the war we're fighting (incarnation versus excarnation), we have no way of properly discerning which side's principles shape our deepest attitudes and daily choices. The determining factor is whether we live the body as something *symbolic* or *diabolic*. In the Greek, *symballein* means to bring together, unite. *Diaballein* means to throw apart, rupture.

The word "symbol" has a long history with origins in the ability of a broken token—half of a ring is a typical example—to witness, in the absence of its wholeness, to that which can't be seen. Looking at one half of the ring, one knows that the other half is *meant* to be there and one can imagine its shape and presence. Each piece of the ring is *meant* for the other, they *fit* together. Hence, when Saint Paul teaches that the body is *meant* for the Lord, and the Lord is *meant* for the body, he's saying the body is "symbolic." One must not conclude, of course, that God "needs" the body to complete him: God needs nothing. Rather, the body and the Lord/the Lord and the body only make sense

---

43 Nicholas Healy, "The Spirit of Christian Doctrine," *Communio* (Summer 2016), 240.

to us—are only fully revealed *to us*—when the two are brought together and become one, when the two "kiss."

Cut off from the Lord, "the body" becomes crude biological matter, a "meat-suited skeleton" destined for the grave. Cut off from the body, "the Lord" becomes an intangible theological abstraction. However, when the two become one, the body becomes a theophany destined for eternal union with the Trinity, and the mystery of the Lord becomes tangible and communicable in time and space: it is that "which we have seen with our eyes," says Saint John, "and touched with our hands, concerning the Word of life" (1 Jn 1:1). In other words, when the two pieces of the ring that belong together are brought together (the body and the Lord/the Lord and the body), the biological becomes theological and the abstractions of theology become tangible.

But one could retort, "We are two thousand years removed from the 'tangibility' of God-in-the-flesh. Where does God as abstraction become God-in-the-flesh for me, today?" And we find ourselves circling back to what the Church's liturgy purports to offer the world; we find ourselves back at the source and summit of everything the Church believes and proclaims to all who hunger and thirst: namely, that God-in-the-flesh—Absolute Beauty incarnate—is *truly present* in the Eucharist, and we're invited to "take and eat." This means, as Albacete puts it, that every Mass is like the sign on that altar in Nazareth where we encounter "the scaaaaandaaaal of the *HIC!*"[44]

It is the redemptive power of Christ's body in the here and now (*hic et nunc*) that the enemy wants to keep us from experiencing.

---

44 See *Culture at the Crossroads of Reality and Reason: A Collection of Monsignor Lorenzo Albacete's Talks to the Crossroads Advisory Board Meetings* (Crossroads Cultural Center, 2015), 62.

In every Mass, the two pieces of the ring that belong together—the body and the Lord/the Lord and the body—are brought together in the sacrament of the Eucharist: "This is my body, which is given up for you" (Lk 22:19). And the *diabolic* one is hell-bent on preventing such a Holy Communion, such a holy kiss. The *diabolic* one wants to rob us of the *symbolic* meaning of our bodies and of the entire created world.

This is precisely what he's done. Because of the inheritance of original sin, we come into this world with impaired vision. While there's a distant echo in our hearts of a time when we once saw our naked bodies just as God made them to be—as the most pure and brilliant theophany—for the most part, we "look but do not see" (Mt 13:13). The good news is that Christ is in the business of giving sight to the blind. Oh, Lord, open our eyes!

INTO THE MYSTIC

1. What's something you learned in this chapter that you hadn't known before?

2. In what ways have you been "evangelized" by the Gnosticism of the secular world? Have you conceived of Christianity as a flight from the body?

3. Have you ever pondered what it means that the Lord is *meant* for your body and your body is *meant* for the Lord? What impact does that have on your day-to-day life?

4. Have you realized that your body is at the heart and center of a cosmic battle between good and evil? How do you see the war between incarnation and excarnation at work in your own life?

CHAPTER 4

Beauty Bathed In Light

If your whole body is full of light, and no part of it is in darkness, then it will be as full of light as a lamp illuminating you with its brightness.

—JESUS (LK 11:36)

This chapter will unfold the theophany revealed in our bodies when they are bathed in divine light and no part of them is left in darkness. Before we do that, however, let's start with a review. We began our reflections by seeking to name that unnamed yearning we all feel for a Beauty that lasts, a Beauty that never fades. In keeping with the Fathers of the Church, we called it *eros*. In Chapter 2, we reflected on the basic problem of human existence—that, precisely because eros is a hunger for infinite Beauty, we cannot satisfy it on our own. We are entirely dependent on the Infinite One who responds to our hunger by humbling himself to the point of becoming food for us. By feeding on this "bread from heaven," we experience "divinization by digestion."

The carnality of it all brought us to our reflection on the body as the very soul of Christianity.

We must ask ourselves: What kind of creatures *are* we that we experience hunger not just for physical sustenance, but for beauty? Putting words to this profound cry of his heart, a student of mine once marveled, "I don't only want to *behold* the beauty of a sunrise. I want to *eat* it."[1] C.S. Lewis captures this sentiment perceptively in his classic work *The Weight of Glory*:

> We do not want merely to *see* beauty, though, God knows, even that is bounty enough. We want something else which can hardly be put into words—to be united with the beauty we see, to pass into it, to receive it into ourselves, to bathe in it, to become part of it. . . . That is why the poets tell us such lovely falsehoods. They talk as if the west wind could really sweep into a human soul; but it can't. They tell us that "beauty born of murmuring sound" will pass into a human face; but it won't. Or not yet. For if we take the imagery of Scripture seriously, if we believe that God will one day *give* us the Morning Star and cause us to *put on* the splendor of the sun, then we may surmise that . . . [such] poetry, so false as history, may be very near the truth as prophecy. At present we are on the outside of the world, the wrong side of the door. . . . But all the leaves of the New Testament are rustling with the rumor that it will not always be so. Someday, God willing, we shall get *in*.[2]

---

1 This student, Evan Lemoine, to whom I owe a debt of gratitude for the title of this book, has gone on to become an excellent teacher and author in his own right, unpacking the riches of John Paul II's Theology of the Body in both the English- and Spanish-speaking worlds (amaralmaximo.com).

2 *The Weight of Glory* (Harper One, 1980) 42–43.

And let us be careful not to excarnate this "getting *in*." As human persons we can only be reached in our totality through the concrete, and that means *through the reality of our bodies*. Salvation history is the story of the Transcendent Mystery of God becoming more and more concrete for us, to the point that Infinite Beauty takes on flesh and blood in order to sacrifice them as actual food and drink for us, so that such Beauty might truly be *in* us and we might truly be *in* such Beauty: "Whoever eats my flesh and drinks my blood remains *in* me and I *in* him" (Jn 6:56).

To Know God

Prayerfully contemplating that two-letter word "in" will open up an abyss of awe and wonder regarding the depths of the intimacy to which we are invited with God. The Father and the Son live an eternal mystery of blissful, intimate indwelling. The Father "*dwells in me*" says Jesus (Jn 14:10); "you, Father, are *in* me and I *in* you" (Jn 17:21). And their desire is that we would be *in* them as well: Jesus prays that "they may all be one, as you, Father, are *in* me and I *in* you, that they also may be *in* us. . . . And I have given them the glory you gave me, so that they may be one, as we are one, I *in* them and you *in* me, that they may be brought to perfection as one" (Jn 17:21–23).

Every human life begins through a mysterious oneness and bodily indwelling: our parents became "one flesh" through an indwelling bodily exchange that generated us *within* our mother's womb. There—within her body, and her body within ours (in the form of sustenance)—we lived and developed for the first several months of our lives. If it's true that our origin foreshadows our destiny, then somehow the beautiful mystery of our own prenatal indwelling hints at some kind of eternal experience of dwelling *within* infinite

Beauty, and infinite Beauty dwelling *within* us. Jesus speaks to this when he expresses his desire for us to know the love of the Father as he does: "that the love with which you loved me may be *in* them, and I *in* them" (Jn 17:26). Similarly, Jesus reveals the nature of our destiny when he proclaims: "This is eternal life, that they may know you, the only true God, and Jesus Christ whom you have sent" (Jn 17:3).

You'll find these words of John 17:3 at the very start of the *Catechism*. Of all the opening lines that could have been chosen, of all the verses of Scripture that might have been appropriate, the prologue of the *Catechism* begins here. What does the Church want to teach us by announcing these words before all else? Monsignor Albacete reflects:

> Pay attention to one word in that quote. The word is *this*. It's the most important word. . . . Otherwise "eternal life" becomes still another concept . . . another abstract idea. No-no-no-no! *THIS* is eternal life. . . . Eternal life—this is the claim of the Christian Gospel—has appeared concretely, specifically *in the flesh!* It has become a *"this thing."* Not just a concept. Eternal life is found in finding this concrete reality. *THIS* is eternal life.[3]

In keeping with all that we've reflected on up to this point, the very first thing the *Catechism* wants us to consider is the *concreteness* of the Christian proposal as a response that corresponds precisely with the deepest cry of the human heart. To drive the point home, after its prologue, part 1 of the *Catechism* begins with an ode to human *desire* and its *fulfillment*: "The desire for

3   Lorenzo Albacete, *Retrieve* video series, episode 2.

God is written in the human heart, because man is created by God and for God; and God never ceases to draw man to himself. Only in God will he find the truth and happiness he never stops searching for: The dignity of man rests above all on the fact that he is called to communion with God."[4]

Again, we must resist the tendency to abstract, to fly away from the concrete. This is a communion accomplished through our bodies. Let's be more specific: it's accomplished *through our mouths*. The mouth is a primal and primordial source of knowledge. A newborn craves nourishment, comfort, love, and finds them with mouth latched firmly on to mother's breast. And in a few months, how will that infant explore the world? Everything will go right *in* the mouth. To taste and take in is to come to *know*. And although we learn the hard way that there are plenty of things we shouldn't put in our mouths, this desire to take in doesn't disappear with age. In fact, it intensifies with fiery passion!

What are lovers saying with their opened-mouth kisses, if not: "I want to *taste* you, *know* you, take you *in* to myself"? They're saying, quite literally, "I *adore* you." Adoration comes from the Latin *ad-ora*, meaning "at the mouth." In the opening verse of the Song of Songs the bride cries for her bridegroom: "Let him kiss me with the kisses of his mouth!" Reading this erotic love poetry with the mind of the Church, this cry represents the yearning of every human heart for intimate knowledge of God. "The mouth of the Bridegroom," says Saint Gregory of Nyssa, "is the source from which springs the words of eternal life (Jn 6:68): if anyone is thirsty let him come to me and drink (Jn 7:37)!

4   CCC 27.

For this reason the thirsty soul wants to offer its mouth to the mouth from which Life springs by saying, 'Let him kiss me with the kisses of his mouth.'"[5] And "the kiss" the Infinite One gives, as numerous saints have attested, is the Eucharist: "Open wide *your mouth* and I will fill it," says the Lord (Ps 81:11). "For those acquainted with the hidden meaning of the Scriptures," says Gregory, "the invitation to [enter] the mystery that was given to the apostles is identified with that of the Song of Songs: 'Eat, O friends, and drink deeply' . . . and the intoxication is Christ himself."[6]

If the Eucharist is real, then what is my mouth? It is the open gateway by which I take *in* the living God, by which I come to *know* Infinite Love *in* me. And what is my tongue? It is the meeting place of heaven and earth, the fleshy throne of the Most-High God, by which I come to "taste and see that the Lord is good" (Ps 34:9). This is the language of a profound intimacy. This is the language of lovers: "When the body of Christ will touch your lips," says Saint Cyril of Jerusalem, "then the wish of the Bride will be fulfilled for you: let him kiss me with the kisses of his mouth! The unity of love . . . is then consummated."[7] As Saint John Paul II proclaimed: "*The Eucharist is the . . . sacrament of the Bridegroom and of the Bride*." In instituting the Eucharist, Christ "thereby wished to express the relationship between man and woman, between what is 'feminine' and what is 'masculine.' It is a relationship willed by God in both the mystery of creation and in the mystery of Redemption."[8]

5   Saint Gregory of Nyssa, *In Canticum Canticorum*, Homily 1.
6   Ibid., Homily 10.
7   Cited in Blaise Arminjon, *The Cantata of Love: A Verse by Verse Reading of the Song of Songs* (Ignatius Press, 1988), 58.
8   John Paul II, *Mulieris Dignitatem* 26.

The Spousal Meaning of Knowledge

If eternal life is to *know* God, we mustn't forget (or ignore, as some are inclined to do) the spousal significance of that word as it's revealed in Scripture: "Adam *knew* his wife, Eve, and she conceived" (Gen 4:1).[9] The book of Hosea, John Paul II tells us, is one of the first biblical poems to apply the spousal sense of "knowledge" to God's relationship with his people: "I will betroth you to me with fidelity, and you shall *know* the Lord" (Hos 2:22). John Paul II then sketches a brief history of this deeply embedded theme in both Scripture and the theological tradition, observing that it passed from Hosea to Isaiah and Ezekiel, and culminates in Paul's letter to the Ephesians; from there it was developed extensively by the Fathers of the Church and the great mystics, such as John of the Cross, whom the late Polish pope, as his student and spiritual son, mentions by name.[10] Here are some key passages from Isaiah and Ezekiel:

> For as a young man marries a virgin
> So shall your Maker marry you;
> And as the bridegroom rejoices over his bride,
> So shall your God rejoice over you. (Is 62:5)

9   As the Reverend Thomas G. James points out, in the New Testament "the Hebrew word *yada* is replaced in kind with the Greek word *ginosko*." However, it "has all the same meanings in the New Testament that *yada* has in the Old Testament, including sex" (https://wsumc.com/multimedia-archive/yada-ginosko-to-know/).

10 See John Paul II, TOB 21, n32. As a young priest, John Paul II learned Spanish so he could read Saint John of the Cross in his original language. John Paul II's doctoral dissertation in theology was on faith according to John of the Cross.

Your breasts were formed and your hair had grown
You were naked and bare.
When I passed by you again and looked upon you,
Behold, you were at the age for love . . .
I entered into a covenant with you, says the Lord
And you became mine. (Ezek 16:7–8)

While we may need to work through some discomfort or fear to reclaim the true sacredness of the imagery, it's clear that the prophets "described God's passion for his people using boldly erotic images," says Benedict XVI.[11] "These biblical texts indicate that eros is part of God's very Heart," he affirms. Indeed, "the Almighty awaits the 'yes' of his creatures as a young bridegroom that of his bride."[12] To give that "yes," in turn, is to exercise the supreme act of human freedom.

But we can rightly wonder what this imagery might have meant to the people of the Old Testament. How could eros—a yearning we feel and experience bodily—be expressed by a God who is pure Spirit? Only with the Incarnation of the Eternal Bridegroom will this imagery be fulfilled. In the New Testament the "imagery of marriage between God and Israel is now realized in a way previously inconceivable: it had meant standing in God's presence, but now it becomes union with God through sharing in Jesus's self-gift, sharing in his body and blood."[13] We could put it this way: if in the Old Testament, spousal imagery led to a covenantal exchange of vows between God and the chosen people, in the New Testament, the Eternal Bridegroom takes flesh so as to consummate the union.

11 Benedict XVI, *Deus Caritas Est* 9.
12 Benedict XVI, Lenten Message, 2007.
13 Benedict XVI, *Deus Caritas Est* 13.

Quoting directly from Genesis, the Apostle Paul proclaims: "For this reason a man shall leave his father and mother and be joined to his wife, and the two shall become one flesh." For what reason? With daring mystical insight, the apostle proclaims that sexual differentiation and union was a prophecy *right from the beginning* of both the Incarnation and the Eucharist: "This is a great mystery," he says—a *mega* mystery in Greek—"and I mean in reference to Christ and the Church" (Eph 5:31–32). Christ left his Father in heaven to take flesh in the womb of Mary. Then he left the home of his mother to give up that flesh for his Bride, the Church, so that we might become one-in-the-flesh with him. This is why John Paul II calls the Eucharist *"the sacrament of the Bridegroom and of the Bride."*

Here, in the communion of these two holy communions (husband-wife/Christ-Church), we discover the "crowning" of all the themes in Sacred Scripture, John Paul II tells us. We discover the "central reality" in some sense of the whole of divine revelation.[14] The mystery spoken of in this passage "is *'great' indeed*," he says. "It is what God . . . wishes above all to transmit to mankind in his Word." Thus, one can say that this passage linking marital union with Christ's union with the Church "reveals—in a particular way—*man to man himself* and makes *his supreme vocation* clear."[15]

What is this "supreme vocation"? It is nothing less than bodily participation in the eternal ecstasy of the Trinitarian exchange into which we are "grafted" through the marriage between Christ and the Church. Yes, from this perspective

---

14   See John Paul II, TOB 87:3.
15   Ibid. 87:6; 93:2.

we can say the central reality of the whole of divine revelation is that *God wants to marry us.* This is what the covenants and testaments are all about. The Bible itself starts in Genesis with the nuptials of the first man and woman and concludes in Revelation with the nuptials of Christ and the Church. The beginning foreshadows the end, and these bookends provide the interpretive key for all that lies between.

The Essence of Biblical Faith

Scripture uses many images, of course, to help us understand God's love for us, and each has its own valuable place. But, as John Paul II affirmed, the gift of the heavenly Bridegroom's body on the Cross gives "definitive prominence to the spousal meaning of God's love."[16] The idea of the Cross as the consummation of the divine-human nuptials, in fact, has been a regular theme of the Church's reflection from the time of the ancient Fathers through today. "He came to the marriage bed of the cross," wrote Saint Augustine, "and there in mounting it, he consummated his marriage. And when he perceived the sighs of the creature, he lovingly gave himself up to the torment in place of his bride, and joined himself to her forever."[17] Saint Quodvultdeus, a contemporary of Augustine, uses the same evocative imagery: "Let our Bridegroom ascend the wood of his bridal chamber; let our Bridegroom ascend the wood of his marriage bed." He then elaborates: "Just as when Eve was made from the side of the sleeping Adam, so the Church was formed from the side of Christ, hanging on the cross. . . . How great is the mystery

16   John Paul II, *Mulieris Dignitatem* 26.
17   Augustine, *Sermo Suppositus* 120.

of this Bridegroom and this bride! Human words are not up to explaining it. . . . At the very moment her spouse dies, the bride marries him. . . . At the moment he is raised above the heavens, she is made fruitful throughout the whole earth."[18]

In the same vein, Benedict XVI affirms: "On the cross God's eros for us is made manifest. . . . Is there more 'mad eros' than that which led the Son of God to make himself one with us even to the point of suffering as his own the consequences of our offences?"[19] Our mad thirst for God, once again, is but a dim shadow of his mad thirst for us. And prayer "is the encounter of God's thirst with ours."[20] Prayer, John Paul II tells us, must progress through numerous "painful purifications (the 'dark night'). But it leads, in various possible ways, to the ineffable joy experienced by the mystics as 'nuptial union.'"[21] Why do the mystics love the spousal imagery of the Scriptures? Why have the saints written more commentaries on the Song of Songs than any other book in the Bible? Because they discovered in that divinely inspired erotic love poetry a language expressing their own experience of prayer. They saw in the Song of Songs not only an expression of the intimacies of marital love. They saw also "an expression of the essence of biblical faith: that man can indeed enter into union with God—his primordial aspiration."[22]

Scripture calls this union with God the "Marriage of the Lamb" (Rev 19:7). In fact, the Bible uses the same word—

---

18 Saint Quodvultdeus of Carthage, *The Creedal Homilies* (Newman Press, 2004), 37–38.
19 Benedict XVI, Lenten Message 2007. Benedict credits Eastern mystic Nicholas Cabasilis for the expression "mad eros."
20 CCC 2560.
21 John Paul II, *Novo Millennio Ineunte* 33.
22 Benedict XVI, *Deus Caritas Est* 10.

"to be joined" or "to cling"—to describe both nuptial union and union with God. Jeremiah drew this parallel rather shockingly when he proclaimed with a prophetic "thus says the Lord" insistence: "As closely as the loincloth clings to a man's loins, so I desire the whole house of Israel and the whole house of Judah to cling to me." Then he laments, "But they did not listen" (Jer 13:11). Do we? Do we even know *how* to listen to such a flabbergasting call to intimacy with God, or are we just disturbed by such imagery?

If human sexuality is the first school of religion, as we observed in the previous chapter, it would seem we've been flunking out ever since the dawn of sin and the entrance of shame (see Gen 3:7). That's when we started allowing *the wrong voice* to form our view of our bodies: "Who told you that you were naked?" (Gen 3:11). The voice of the one who created us "naked without shame" and called the two to become "one flesh" wants us to know that he did so to be a sign, an icon, a symbol, an analogy here on earth of heavenly realities. While it's obvious, as John Paul II affirms, that God's "*mystery* remains *transcendent with respect to this analogy* as with respect to any other analogy." At the same time, when we let the sign of spousal love and union split open, it offers a certain "penetration" into the very essence of the divine mystery.[23] Yes, our bodies—precisely in the mystery of sexual differentiation, union, and fertility—are a theophany! They proclaim the mystery that God is an eternal exchange of Life-giving Love. Our bodies—precisely in the mystery of sexual differentiation, union, and fertility—are *far* from meaningless. They have a *spousal* meaning that tells the story

23 John Paul II, TOB 95b:1.

of *God's* spousal love: the story that God loves us, wants to marry us, and wants us to conceive eternal life within us.

The Mystery of Mary as Virgin-Bride-Mother

This is not merely a metaphor. Representing all of us, a young Jewish woman once gave her "yes" to God's marriage proposal with such totality and fidelity that she literally conceived eternal life in her womb. In a hymn addressed to the Mother of God, Saint Augustine exclaims: "The Word becomes united with flesh, he makes his covenant with flesh, and your womb is the sacred bed on which this holy union of the Word with flesh is consummated."[24] Although Mary did "not know man" (Lk 1:34), at the moment of the Incarnation, Hosea's prophecy —"you shall know the Lord" (Hos 2:22)—was superabundantly fulfilled in her. In "the pages of the Annunciation . . . the New Covenant is presented to us as the Nuptial Covenant of God with man, of divinity with humanity," as Saint John Paul II observes. "God's nuptial love, announced by the prophets, is concentrated on [Mary] perfectly and definitively. She is also the virgin-bride to whom it is granted conceiving and bearing forth the Son of God: *the unique fruit of the nuptial love of God toward humanity*, represented and summarized comprehensively as it were in Mary."[25]

Mary's virginity is not a negation of sexual union. Rather, it reveals the ultimate reality to which sexual union points: Mary's virginity reveals her to be the "mystic bride of love

---

24 Augustine, Sermon 291.
25 John Paul II, "The Holy Spirit and Mary: Model of the Nuptial Union of God with Humanity," General Audience of May 2, 1990 (this is a private translation as no official English translation exists).

eternal."[26] As French philosopher Fabrice Hadjadj explains, "Mary's virginity is not a rejection of sexuality as is frequently thought, but, on the contrary, its most perfect fulfillment. Mary is not asexual, but a woman made of blood and bone." Sexuality properly understood "is above all an opening onto transcendence. It is, which is especially important here, a fertile opening. It enters into a drama and this drama is connected with being fruitful. In Mary this opening is radical. She reveals that the essence of sexuality is not a passing pleasure, but being open to . . . God himself." Hence, Hadjadj concludes that "in the case of Mary we are dealing with the revelation of the very essence of sexuality."[27]

We tend to shy away even from mentioning the word "sexuality" in reference to Mary, as if our own disordered experiences thereof were all that ever existed or could exist. Rather than imagining an immaculate experience of eros and sexuality opened to the divine, we dehumanize Mary with our false piety and our excarnate vision of "holiness." Hans Urs von Balthasar insists that there's no getting away from Mary's fertile, feminine flesh if we are to do justice to the mystery of the Incarnation. Mary conceives through an act of faith, but the very fact that this happens *in her womb*— through her fertile, feminine flesh—indicates that faith must penetrate "down to the foundation of matter . . . down to the deepest fibers of [her] flesh. If these fibers were not in echoing readiness," reflects Balthasar, "how could the Word become flesh? If it becomes flesh, it has to emerge from the

---

26 This expression is taken from the hymn "Holy Light on Earth's Horizon" by Fr. Edward Caswall (1814–1878).
27 "Sexuality as Transcendence: An Interview with Fabrice Hadjadj," ethikapolitika.org, April 14, 2015.

deepest foundations of life. And this deepest depth has to receive the Word . . . with the active readiness with which a feminine womb receives the masculine seed."[28]

This means that "Mary is not simply an inert locus of the event," as Father Jean Corbon expresses it. She provides a truly feminine/bridal energy of acceptance in which "her entire being as a person is offered, given, handed over to the Holy Spirit." In the language of the Eastern Fathers, Mary's bridal opening to the divine "Energy" (the "river of life" that flows from the eternal Father) leads to a "synergy" (a combining of energies) between Creator and creature that generates the God-Man in the depths of her virginal womb. Corbon continues: "Now indeed joy erupts! . . . The coming of the eternal mystery shakes our death-marked time and causes it to gape open."[29]

Again, we must insist that Mary's virginity does not deny or negate eros. Rather, in its utterly gaped-open surrender to the eternal "river of life" (divine eros), Mary's virginity liberates human eros from its link with death. "It has always been recognized," observes Olivier Clement, "from the ancient myths down to Freud himself, that love and death, *eros* and *thanatos* [Greek for "death"], are inseparable.[30] In Mary's virginal motherhood, her fruitful virginity, we see transcendence intervening to snatch love out of the hands of death . . . setting in motion the universal transfiguration."[31] It is in Mary that the bride's dream for a love that is "stronger than death" comes true.

28 Hans Urs von Balthasar, *Mary: The Church at the Source*, p. 162.
29 Corbon, *The Wellspring of Worship*, 38–39.
30 This basic intuition stems from the innate (though not always conscious) realization that, in as much as erotic love gives rise to the next generation, it also portends the end (the death) of the current one.
31 Olivier Clement, *The Roots of Christian Mysticism*, 42.

Making Visible the Invisible

Once again, the divine plan to conquer death and bring life "to the full" is revealed and made possible in and through the human body in the mystery of the sexual difference. Hence, the person who faithfully accepts the Christian proposal instinctively knows that an attack against the God-given meaning of the body, gender, sexuality, and marriage is an attack not only against human life, but against the revelation of the divine Life. God, of course, is not sexual. In himself, "God is pure spirit in which there is no place for the difference between the sexes."[32] But the sexual difference in us presents a call to life-giving communion that echoes the Trinity's own Life-giving Communion within the created order, thus making that which is *not-God* (creation) a suitable dwelling place for that which *is-God*. Here's how Albacete explains it:

> Jesus Christ, he who is the eternal Son of the Father's Love, as a divine Person, is always in relationship. So, this world that is not-God must still be capable of sustaining free relationships [as opposed to instinctual relationships, as is the case among animals], because otherwise Jesus Christ cannot, like, "fit" in [this world], you see. He's not an isolated individual, never ever. Look at the Bible: "Father, I know that you always hear me, you're always with me," etc. . . . . The world, creation, if it is *for* Christ, must be a reality where a personal relationship of communion is possible; where *Love* is possible. The world is created so that *the world itself* is capable of Love, so that it can be the home of Jesus Christ.

---

32 CCC 370; the second Person of the Trinity, however, having taken on a male body, is sexual in this sense.

The summit of the created world is the human being . . .
not as an isolated individual, but as a communion between
persons. . . . The very *first* communion—in the story of
Genesis you see it—male and female. It is a real communion
between others. It cannot be [between two people who are]
the same . . . otherwise you're loving a projection of yourself. You love the radically *other.* So what you call "man,"
the human person, the human being, must exist in a polar-
ity like this—totally as male, totally as female—so that the
love between the two forms, that interpersonal communion
that serves as the ground, if you wish, for the Son of God to
enter into his world, to be the first among many, to be the
center and the head of *all* creation, by embracing into the
relationship that he lives, the Father and the Son—into the
relationship that he *is*—the relationship among human persons that is love. That is the *secret* of sexual differentiation.
Sexual differentiation is a sign, a word, a message that says:
Jesus Christ, Jesus Christ.[33]

What an astounding declaration! Here Albacete asserts that
the ultimate purpose of the entire visible world, all of which
culminates in our creation *as male and female*, is to make the
Incarnation possible. If this is true, then the ultimate purpose of
"femaleness"—of female fertility, of woman's womb, of motherhood—is to be the portal that gives heaven entrance to earth,
making the Incarnation possible. And the ultimate purpose of
"maleness"—of male potency, of fatherhood—is so that the eternal Son could take human flesh that properly signified the mystery of the eternal Father and the potency of his love: "Whoever

---

33 Lorenzo Albacete, *Retrieve* video series, episode 6.

has seen me has seen the Father" (Jn 14:9). In short, Albacete is asserting that the ultimate purpose of the sexual difference is the fulfillment of this petition of the "Our Father": thy kingdom come, thy will be done *on earth as it is in heaven*—a prayer that "earth no longer differ from heaven."[34] If heaven *is* the eternal generation of the Son by the Father (between whom is shared the love that *is* the Holy Spirit), then the petition "on earth as it is in heaven" is superabundantly fulfilled when the eternal Son is generated within time in Mary's womb.

At the moment of her "yes" to heaven's invitation, Isaiah's prophecy is fulfilled: "Let justice descend, you heavens, like dew from above. . . . Let the earth open and salvation bud forth" (Is 45:8). Mary's womb has become that "open earth" that has been "filled with the *knowledge* of the Lord" (Is 11:9), that "open earth" that no longer differs from heaven!

Precisely here, in the mystery of Mary's virginal conception of Christ, we encounter the rich iconography of maleness and femaleness. The male body is the icon of the Creator's longing to enter his creation; the female body is the icon of the creature's longing to be "filled with all the fullness of God" (Eph 3:19). In Mary's female body pregnant with Christ's male body, these longings of the Creator and the creature embrace in superabundant, mutual fulfillment. "Motherhood," observes John Paul II, has thus "been introduced into the order of the Covenant that God made with humanity in Jesus Christ. Each and every time that *motherhood* is repeated in human history, it is always *related to the Covenant* which God established with the human race through the motherhood of the Mother of God."[35]

---

34 CCC 2825.

35 John Paul II, *Mulieris Dignitatem* 19.

Hence, in and through the eyes of faith, we can recognize, as John Paul II affirms, that whenever spouses open themselves to the grace of their sacrament, putting that biblical "knowledge" at the service of generation (or, at least, the possibility thereof), they are forming "a *sign that* efficaciously *transmits in the visible world the invisible mystery hidden in God from eternity.* And this is the mystery of Truth and Love, the mystery of divine life, in which man really participates."[36]

This is what makes the human body not only bio-logical, but theo-logical: it reveals not only the logic of the living human organism; it reveals the logic of the divine life—eternal life. As we have been emphasizing, eternal life is something concrete, tangible. It's not just a concept; through the Incarnation, eternal life has become a "this thing." It can be sensed, touched, felt, seen, experienced. As Saint John says, we "proclaim to you the eternal life that was with the Father and was made visible to us" (1 Jn 1:2)—visible *through the body.* "The body, in fact, and only the body," John Paul II insists, "is capable of making visible what is invisible: the spiritual and the divine."[37] For *this* reason the two will become one flesh: to be a sign revealing the logic of God, the logic of the Incarnation, the "mega mystery" that the *Logos* has become one in the flesh with us (see Eph 5:31–32). As Timothy Patitsas observes, our sexed bodies "function as an icon with eternal significance. And they are beautiful—deeply and permanently beautiful—as well, since their very reality is attained in their becoming symbols of heaven."[38] Christianity is the invitation to develop

---

36 John Paul II, TOB 19:4; see also TOB 23 for his reflections on "knowledge" and generation.

37 Ibid.

38 Patitsas, "Chastity and Empathy," 29.

this sensibility, this ability to *sense* our bodies (understood as the summation of the entire physical world) as icons with eternal significance, symbols of heaven.

For this to happen, however, Jesus says each person must bring his or her body into the light so that "no part of it is in darkness." If we venture along the way of allowing all diseased (dis-eased) images and ideas about the meaning of our bodies to be burned up in the fire of his healing, merciful love, then our bodies "will be as full of light as a lamp illuminating [us] with its brightness" (Lk 11:36). When we prefer shadows and darkness, however, our bodies lose their logic; they become nonsensical. Tragically, today, not only has the modern world lost *all sense* of our bodies' supernatural meaning, even the natural meaning of being male and female has been rendered invisible. That, of course, is the end game of excarnating spirits: to blind us to the natural meaning of the body so as to eclipse its supernatural meaning. As Christ laments to Nicodemus, "If I tell you about earthly things and you do not believe, how will you believe if I tell you about heavenly things?" (Jn 3:12). It's very simple: the Holy Spirit moves to make what is invisible *visible in the flesh* (incarnation), while evil spirits move to make what is visible in the flesh *invisible* (excarnation), so that we "look but do not see" (Mt 13:13). One of their essential goals in this physical world is to blind us to theophany.

Immediately after Jesus probes our hearts with that most essential question, *"What do you want?"* he invites us to the healing of our blindness: "Come," he says, "and you will see." Or, more accurately, *"Come, and become one who sees"* (Jn 1:39). Jesus wants to "un-anesthetize" us, making us alive and sensitive to the theophanies happening in us and around us all the time. "Follow me," Jesus is saying, "and I will make the invisible visible. Follow me and I will open your eyes to all the beauty within you and around you—and even more, to all the Beauty behind all that beauty." Unless we develop this sensibility to beauty's ability to reveal Beauty (theophany/sacramentality), unless we become one who *sees*, we will never *know* (in the biblical sense of that word) what we want.

"Jesus, Son of David, have mercy on me . . . I want to see!" (Lk 18:38, 41).

INTO THE MYSTIC

1. What's something you learned in this chapter that you hadn't known before?

2. Have you ever pondered your mouth and tongue as the meeting place of heaven and earth? What fears or discomforts arise when you think of addressing these words to God: "Kiss me with the kisses of your mouth"? Pour your heart out to the Lord just as you find it, and listen to how he might be speaking to you.

3. Have you ever considered the Cross as Christ's "marriage bed," where God pours out his "mad eros" for each human heart? What obstacles might you need to work through in your own heart to enter more deeply into these mysteries?

4. Are there parts of your body, or memories surrounding certain parts of your body, that remain in the dark? If so, write down those memories in a letter to Jesus, and listen for his response. He was with you in the events that created these memories and he knows how to untwist whatever sin (your own and/or the sin of others) has twisted up.

CHAPTER 5

Beauty Buried In Darkness

The lamp of the body is the eye. If your eye . . . is bad,
your whole body will be in darkness.
And if the light in you is darkness,
how great will the darkness be.

—JESUS (MT 6:22–23)

In the last chapter we learned that, while everything God created is a theophany, since our creation as male and female is the crown of creation, it is also the crown of theophanies. All that exists reflects something of the beauty of the Creator, but only the human being has the honor and dignity of being created in the image and likeness of God. This divine image is revealed not only in the fact that we have reason and free will. These were given to us as the power to love, as the power to enter into genuine relationships of communion with other persons. The *Catechism* observes that "as image of God we live in relation." This means that the "communion of the Holy Trinity is the source and criterion of truth in every relationship."[1] Human relationships flourish in as much as they image the loving exchange among the Trinity, and they flounder in as much as they do not.

In one of the most important teachings of the Second Vatican Council, we read that when Jesus "prayed to the Father 'that all may be one . . . as we are one' (Jn 17:21–22), . . . he implied a certain likeness between the union of divine Persons and the unity of God's children in truth and love. It follows then," the Council observes, "that if man is the only creature on earth that God willed for its own sake, man can only find himself through the sincere gift of self."[2] Because of our dignity as creatures endowed with reason and free will, we feel violated when we are treated as a tool for someone else's sake. This can happen in any number of ways; for example, in a job in which we are treated merely as a means for making someone else money, or in a relationship (sexual or otherwise) in which we are used according to the whim or desire of another. The violation we feel in such situations reveals that we are created for our *own sake*. However, we're not meant to live for our own sake. Because we are made in the image of God, who, as a Trinity of Persons lives an eternal exchange of self-giving love, we are meant to live for others, becoming a gift to them and receiving the gift of others in a mutually enriching, life-giving communion of persons.

As we've been learning, the fundamental human expression of this giving and receiving/receiving and giving is meant to be realized in the relationship of man and woman. The call to love as God loves was chiseled by God right in

1   CCC 2563, 2845.
2   *Gaudium et Spes* 24.

the sexual difference. A man's body makes no sense by itself, nor does a woman's body. But seen in light of each other—unless those excarnating spirits have rendered the visible invisible to us—we discover the spousal meaning of the body, which refers to the body's *"power to express love: precisely that love in which the human person becomes a gift* and—through this gift—fulfills the very meaning of his being and existence."[3] Man and woman are literally *organized* by God for one another, which is to say, they have the *organs* that allow them to become one functioning *organism* in the "great mystery" of becoming "one flesh" and generating new life. In this way, as Saint John Paul II tells us, the human body, precisely through its visible masculinity and femininity, becomes an icon that transfers into the visible reality of the world the mystery hidden from eternity in God.[4]

Divine Iconography

Icons are earthly windows to heaven. Just as windows let sunlight into our homes, the sexual difference/communion allows the light of that "mystery hidden from eternity in God" to enter the visible world. By way of review, that mystery refers, first of all, to who God is in himself—to the blissful, intimate indwelling in the Holy Spirit of the Father and the Son: "you, Father, are *in* me and I *in* you" (Jn 17:21). Secondly, and especially exciting for us (because it's *everything* we yearn for), that mystery refers to the invitation God extends to us—the "marriage proposal"—to become "one flesh" with his Eternal Son and thereby be grafted into

---

3   John Paul II, TOB 15:1.
4   See ibid. 19:4.

the infinite ecstasy of the Trinitarian exchange (this happens here and now through the sacraments as a pledge of eternal fulfillment in the resurrection of our glorified bodies).

This invitation to participate in the infinite ecstasy of divine Love *is* the Gospel. It *is* the good news of Christianity. Despite every impression to the contrary, and despite the many counterwitnesses to this truth throughout Christian history, this is the *one* aim, the *one* goal, the *one* purpose for which the Catholic Church exists: to lead the world into the ecstasy of these eternal nuptials.[5] Saint Paul, one of the first apostles of this good news, said it was his mission in life to make this "mystery hidden from eternity in God" plain to everyone, to bring it to light so that others could sense, see, encounter, and experience the "inscrutable riches" of the divine life, so that even we today could *know* "the breadth and length and height and depth" of the love "that surpasses knowledge" and "be filled with all the fullness of God" (Eph 3:8–9, 18–19).

We encountered this last expression in the previous chapter, but may I invite you here to pause and prayerfully take that in? *To be filled with all the fullness of God . . . ?!*

This is the answer the Infinite One gives to the hunger of the human heart for infinite satisfaction: he gives us the sincere gift of *himself* as food to take *into* our deepest selves. In the very design of our humanity we find "a womb-like emptiness," says Peter Kreeft, "crying out to be filled, impregnated by our divine lover."[6] In Mary, it happened. Her womb was literally filled *with all the fullness of God.* "From this point of view,"

---

5   See CCC 772–773.
6   Peter Kreeft, *Heaven, the Heart's Deepest Longing* (Ignatius Press, 1980), 35.

John Paul II tells us, Mary, "the 'woman' is the representative and the archetype of the whole human race: she *represents the humanity* which belongs to all human beings, both men and women."[7] To be human means to open to receive divine love, conceive divine love, and bear it forth for others. That's the theophany of a woman's body. "In fact, there is present in the 'womanhood' of a woman . . . a kind of inherent 'prophecy,' a powerful evocative symbolism, a highly significant 'iconic character' that finds its full realization in Mary and that also aptly expresses the very essence of the Church as . . . the '*bride*' of Christ."[8]

Similarly, there is an inherent prophecy and symbolism in the manhood of a man that finds its full realization in Jesus Christ. His body "given up for us" and his lifeblood "poured out for us" as Bridegroom is the perfect theophany of the Fatherhood of God which fills the Bride (the Church) with "every perfect gift from above" (Js 1:17), enabling the Church through these mystical nuptials to become Mother of all the children regenerated "by water and the Spirit" (Jn 3:5).

It couldn't be of greater significance that Jesus bases entrance into the heavenly realm on a new form of birth from a new form of nuptials. "How can a person be born anew?" Nicodemus wonders. "Surely he cannot enter his mother's womb a second time, can he" (Jn 3:4)? Through the Lord's beautiful and tender providence, Nicodemus finds the answer to his incredulous question when he was granted the honor (along with Joseph of Arimathea) of placing Christ's body in the tomb, which a few days later would reveal itself

---

7   John Paul II, *Mulieris Dignitatem* 4.
8   John Paul II, *Letter to Women* 11.

as the glorious womb of a new birth. Christ was born from a virginal womb and he was born again from a virginal tomb. As John reports, no one had been laid there prior to Jesus (see Jn 19:41). John also observes that Christ's burial coverings were left behind (see Jn 20:5-7), which signifies that "Christ's body had escaped the bonds of death and corruption."[9] Countless biblical commentators have observed the parallel: on Easter morning, the New Adam came out of the ground in a garden (a biblical image of woman's womb) just as the first Adam had—naked without shame (see Gen 2:25). In the resurrected Christ, creation is now restored to the purity of its origins.[10]

This is the astounding nuptial mystery into which we are plunged in the baptismal font. Theodore of Antioch, a fifth-century bishop, observes that just as in our natural birth "the mother's womb receives a seed, but the hand of God fashions it, so in baptism the water becomes a womb for the one who is being born, but the grace of the Spirit fashions the baptized in a second birth."[11] It is here, affirms the *Catechism*, "in the womb of the Church" that "the 'imperishable seed' of the Word of God produces its life-giving effect."[12] It is here in the baptismal font that grace perfects nature and the nuptials of creation find their fulfillment in the nuptials of redemption.

The truth that *grace perfects nature* synthesizes in some way the entire logic of the Christian mystery. But only by pressing into the etymology of the word "nature" do we actually

9   CCC 657.
10 See CCC 2336
11 Theodore of Antioch/Mopsuestia, *Catechetical Homilies*, 14.9, cited in Clement, *The Roots of Christian Mysticism*, 105
12 CCC 2040, 1228.

encounter the basic truth this profound synthesis asserts. "Nature" comes from the Latin *natus*, "born" and *nasci*, "to be born." *That*, fundamentally, is what grace perfects: the most *natural* reality of having been born from the union of our parents. Perfecting, elevating, even divinizing this reality, grace enables us to be "born not by natural generation . . . but of God" (Jn 1:13) through the spousal union of Christ and the Church. Here the "mega mystery" of Ephesians 5 splits open and the logic of this evocative statement of the *Catechism* becomes clear: "The entire Christian life bears the mark of the spousal love of Christ and the Church. Already Baptism, the entry into the People of God, is a nuptial mystery; it is so to speak the nuptial bath which precedes the wedding feast, the Eucharist."[13]

To recognize the divine iconography of the body is to recognize that the mystery of sexual difference proclaims the Gospel itself. *This* is how the apostle Paul makes the divine mystery "plain to everyone" (Eph 3:9), by showing us that an image of it is stamped right in our bodies as male and female and in the call of the two to become "one flesh," in the call to fatherhood and motherhood: "*This* is a mega mystery, and it refers to Christ and the Church" (Eph 5:31–32). The mystery of God indwelling our humanity is not a lesson in theological abstraction; it's a lesson in the *theology of the body*. Building on what we said in the previous chapter about the ultimate purpose of femaleness, a woman's ovaries witness to the human capacity to conceive Christ within as our hope of eternal life: "the mystery hidden from ages and generations past . . . is Christ *in* you, the hope of glory" (Col 1:26–27). This makes

13   Ibid. 1617.

a woman's womb a witness to heaven, the dwelling place of the Lord—or, at least, that's what it's *meant* to be. In turn, as we glimpsed in the last chapter, a man's testicles are a testimony to the eternal Fatherhood of God—or, at least, that's what they are *meant* to be (the very word "testicles" shares the same root as the words *testimony, testify, testament*). As the *Catechism* proclaims, "The *union of man and woman* in marriage is a way of imitating in the flesh the Creator's generosity and fecundity."[14] And John Paul II affirms that although generation "in God is 'totally different,' that is, completely spiritual and divine in essence," nonetheless "every element of human generation which is proper to man, and every element which is proper to woman . . . bears within itself a likeness to, or analogy with the divine 'generating'" in which the eternal life of the Trinity consists.[15]

In short, here, in the entire reality of our creation as male and female that culminates in the call to "be fruitful and multiply" (Gen 1:28), we discover the primordial symbol/icon/sacrament/theophany of eternal life. Only do not mistake the symbol for the symbolized! Do not mistake the earthly portion of the broken ring for the heavenly portion it portends. Not everyone is called to marriage and procreation. In fact, Christ will call some specifically to forgo the earthly symbol of the heavenly reality in order to witness in another way to that mystical union and fertility to which all *are* called in "the Marriage of the Lamb" (see Mt 19:12). In the consummation of those eternal nuptials, the symbol will give way to the ultimate reality to which it was pointing us

---

14   Ibid. 2335.
15   John Paul II, *Mulieris Dignitatem* 8.

all along. At this point, as Christ himself foretold, the sacrament of marriage will come to an end (see Mt 22:30).

Tragically, when we lose our sensibility to the theophany of the sexual difference and its call to fruitful union, we often expect the *window to heaven* to do for us what only *heaven itself* can do: satisfy eros. At this point, the icon degenerates into an idol. It takes a few generations, but any culture that goes down the road of idolizing sex and sexuality, after the initial burst of excitement provided by unbridled indulgence, will eventually come to resent the heck out of the body and the sexual difference for failing to deliver the happiness that culture wrongly sought in them. Unless grace intervenes, future generations—bearing the accumulated fallout of their parents' and grandparents' sexual dysfunction—will collectively despise what their ancestors idolized. We'll explore the pathway from idolizing to despising the body and the sexual difference in the next chapter. It's a journey into a hellish darkness that begins with the loss of the light of theophany, which we'll explore in the remainder of this chapter.

The Original Loss of Theophany

Before sin entered the world, in one of the most evocative lines in all of Sacred Scripture, we read that "the man and his wife were both naked, yet they felt no shame" (Gen 2:25). This biblical detail, which may at first seem cursory, couldn't be more essential in helping us understand the original fullness of our humanity as God designed it to be.[16] The biblical story of our origins presents to us a time of innocence, before the blindness of sin was introduced, in which man and woman *knew* and *experienced* their naked humanity, and all of

16 See John Paul II, TOB 11:2.

creation, as one gloriously harmonious theophany. Imagine seeing, knowing, and rejoicing wholeheartedly and nakedly, without any trace of inner conflict, in the divine sense of humor, in all the poetic beauty and symphonic wonder of the created order!

Deep in our own hearts, beneath our wounds, beneath our defenses, beneath our cynicism, lies the echo of our original innocence. It's almost like an ancient ancestral memory of a time when our first parents, with senses wide open, saw, heard, smelled, tasted, and felt in all the life-givingness of nature—in every bubbling brook, in every blade of grass, in every flower, bush, and tree, in every bird song, cricket chirp, and buzzing bee—the echo of God's Life-giving Love. And they knew and experienced that nature's wondrously erotic love song culminated in their own creation in the image of God *as male and female* and the call to be fruitful and multiply (see Gen 1:27–28). In this mysterious "beginning," man and woman lived and experienced eros as an unfettered celebration of all that is true, good, and beautiful, without any tendency to dominate, use, control, or selfishly grasp at the beauty in which they rejoiced—not least of which was the beauty they saw in themselves and in each other. In short, nakedness without shame demonstrates that *eros* was penetrated and permeated with all the divine radiance and power of *agape*.

Imagine the scene of man and woman in this "paradise of fertile delights" (that's what the word "eden" basically means) as if it were a vibrantly colored, 3-D, high-definition movie with an enthralling score that lifted your heart to the heavens. Then imagine that at the peak of all that enchantment, the movie suddenly collapsed into a two-dimensional blurry black and white with a cacophonic soundtrack grating against your soul. The jolt of that loss is just a shadow of the traumatic horror of the moment when shame shattered their original harmony with God, within themselves, with each other, and with the whole created world.

Sin involved a turning of their hearts away from God, and with that, eros lost its bearings and was turned back on itself. From gen-*eros*-ity in giving and receiving love in the image of God, eros degenerated into a base, selfish urge to use and consume (lust). The theophany in which they had lived and danced and rejoiced so effortlessly was suddenly obscured by a radically different vision. In fact, with the entrance of sin, we read that "the eyes of both of them were opened" to some other view of themselves and the world. Suddenly "they knew that they were naked; so they sewed fig leaves together and made loincloths for themselves" (Gen 3:7). Having lost that divine sense of humor that illuminates the sacramentality of the world as a symbol of heaven, they *looked* at each other but they no longer *saw* the divine mystery revealed through their bodies.

It's not that their bodies suddenly lost their iconic character; they didn't cease to be a window to heaven. Rather, sin pulled the blinds over the window and the heavenly light—although still shining—was almost completely blocked from their vision. We say "almost" because, as John Paul II tells us, that original spousal meaning of the body has not become totally foreign to our hearts because of sin, it is only habitually threatened.[17] It's precisely because of that "habitual threat" that we instinctively feel the need to cover our bodies. We do so in this fallen world not because our bodies themselves are "shameful." We do so

---

17 See Ibid 32:3.

to protect the original goodness and dignity of the body from the degradation of lust. Indeed, our hearts have become a battlefield between love and lust. The more lust dominates our hearts, the less we see our bodies as a theophany.[18]

Tragically, this loss of *seeing* and the battle to reclaim it have become for men and women throughout all of history the "new normal." Inasmuch as this blindness indicates the entrance of sin into the world, this blindness is at the root of all human suffering, of all the dark tragedies the human heart has ever known. But here's our hope; here's our salvation: Christ "came into the world as light" (Jn 12:46). And that light is the glory of God radiating *through his body*. When Jesus says, "If your whole body is full of light and no part of it is in darkness, then your body will be full of light illuminating you with its brightness" (Lk 11:36), he's calling us to what he already lives. For our bodies also to be full of light, we must take the light of his body into our bodies, becoming "one body" with him. And to the degree that we allow the Eucharist to have its way with us, what will the fruit be? Our eyes will become sound again: "When your eye is sound, then your whole body is filled with light, but when it is not sound, then your body is in darkness. Take care that the light in you not become darkness" (Lk 11:34–35).

Like the disciples walking with Jesus on the road to Emmaus, we begin our journey in the dark, unable to recognize the Light of the World right in our midst. But what happens as they stay the journey? "Their hearts are transformed . . . and at the breaking of the bread they experience in reverse fashion what happened to Adam and Eve when they ate from

18 See Ibid.

the fruit of the tree of the knowledge of good and evil; their eyes are opened."[19] They are no longer merely *looking* at externals; they *see* the theophany of the body in the Eucharist and realize it was the Light of the World who had been with them the whole time.

We will discuss the purifications necessary as we walk our own "road to Emmaus" later in these meditations. For now, as we continue exploring how we lost the theophany of our bodies, let us never forget that, however dark our own darkness may be, hope has arisen, allowing us to come back into the light. The absolute Beauty revealed in Christ's body was itself buried in the darkness of the tomb. But in his glorious Resurrection the light of his body shown in the darkness, and the darkness did not overcome it (see Jn 1:5).

The Modern Loss of Theophany

The modern loss of theophany, of course, has its roots in the original loss since all darkness in the human heart can ultimately be traced to the original fall from grace. However, what's new about the modern loss of theophany is that it has happened *after* the light of Christ appeared in history. Indeed, the very nations that once proclaimed the light of the Incarnation to the rest of the world are now imposing the darkness of a radical excarnation on other nations through an "ideological colonization"[20] that robs the body, sex, gender, marriage, and the family of all meaning.

19 Joseph Ratzinger, *Spirit of the Liturgy* (Ignatius Press, 2000), pp. 120–121.
20 This is a term used by Pope Francis to describe a form of oppression of developing societies by affluent ones through imposing an alien worldview on those poorer societies, making adoption of this foreign worldview a condition of humanitarian or developmental aid.

How has this happened? "This is the verdict," says Jesus, "the light came into the world, but people preferred darkness to light" (Jn 3:19). That's the short answer. As the faults and failings of Christians throughout history have made abundantly clear, the restoration of sight that Christ offers has never been automatic. Nor does the healing simply accumulate from generation to generation since each person must be invited to take up the Gospel anew: "We are always having to clear the paths/they will be overgrown again," as John Paul II reflects in one of his poems.[21] Christian history offers countless examples of those who *have* taken up the call and become authentic witnesses to the light of Christ. But it also tells the sad tale of those who bore the badge of Christianity but preferred darkness to light. The witness of the former keeps the Church alive even as she passes through severe trials, while the counterwitness of the latter has contributed significantly to modern revolutions against Christianity.

To the degree that we've reclaimed the divine light of theophany, we'll perceive the faith as it truly is: a call out of darkness that leads to being *seized by Beauty* and *enraptured by God's "mad eros."* To the degree that we remain in the dark, we'll perceive Christianity as a lifeless acceptance of cold, dry doctrines and the imposition of seemingly arbitrary rules that appear to rob us of the very zest of life and all hope of fulfilling eros. When Christianity is perceived as such and imposed on others as such, it's only a matter of time before repressed eros explodes in a cultural revolution that shakes off those shackles in favor of an unbridled indulgence in all manner of sexual vices.

21 John Paul II, *The Place Within*, 170.

The modern sexual revolution, however, is rooted in prior revolutions, especially the scientific revolution, which was born out of the Enlightenment. The "Enlightenment" did, indeed, enlighten us with regard to an understanding of the natural world and the workings of the human body. For all the countless medical, scientific, and technological advantages living in the twenty-first century offers us, we owe the Enlightenment a tremendous debt of gratitude. However, when it comes to the deeper symbolic, prophetic, and iconic meanings of the natural world and of the human body, the "Enlightenment" has left us in the dark.

The scientific and technological mentality is good and necessary for scientific and technological endeavors. As Albacete used to say, "I definitely want my pilot and my surgeon to have a scientific and technological mind." But when we reduce all that can be known to what science can tell us, we become deaf and blind to sacramental presence. We no longer hear the eternal love song that creation is singing. We no longer perceive the Beauty behind the beauty of the redbud tree. We no longer perceive the divine light emanating from the "mega mystery" of sexuality. In fact, we come to oppose that light and the challenges with which it confronts our fallen nature, in favor of the immediate gratification of an inverted eros fixated on maximizing sensual pleasures in the here and now. From within this fixation, any invitation to redirect eros toward something transcendent can only be perceived as a threat to one's "happiness."

With his famous dictum "God is dead," Nietzsche predicted in the late nineteenth century that the "time is coming when man will no longer shoot the arrow of his longing beyond

man."[22] Following in Nietzsche's footsteps, in his 1936 book
The Sexual Revolution, Wilhelm Reich stated quite explicitly
that the goal of the revolution he wanted to inspire was to
replace the religious sense of eros as a desire for the Infinite
with the scientific view that erotic stirrings are merely
physical "excitations" that come from "bioelectric processes
in the tissues." Indeed, Reich insisted that what we think are
religious yearnings are in fact a "vegetative function, which
[man] shares with all living nature" and which "strives for
development, activity, and pleasure. . . in the form of flowing,
surging sensations." His revolution did not need to fight
religion directly, he said. Rather, it just needed to secure "the
sexual happiness of the masses" via the findings of modern
science and then the need for religion would disappear. There
was just one little problem with this approach to "sexual
happiness": in the process of attaining it, as Reich himself
unapologetically acknowledged, the "family will disintegrate
irrevocably." He then casually dismisses any need for concern
by naively assuring his readers that any problems arising from
the collapse of the family "will be constantly discussed publicly
and overcome." In Reich's mind, this was the necessary price
to pay for seeing whether "the Church is correct in its assertion
of the supernatural nature of religious feelings."[23]

Nearly a hundred years later, one would be hard-pressed
to find even one societal problem, one element of social
unrest, chaos, and *un*happiness that is not tied directly or
indirectly to the breakdown of the family that Reich and his
followers ushered in via their version of "sexual happiness."

22 Friedrich Nietzsche, *Thus Spoke Zarathustra* (Penguin, 1978), 17.
23 Wilhelm Reich, *The Sexual Revolution: Toward a Self-Regulating Character
    Structure* (Farrar, Straus and Giroux, 1946), 279.

Carlo Lancellotti observes that the denial of the religious sense of eros is truly paradigmatic of the sexual revolution as "an epochal phenomenon." He maintains that the sexual revolution "is not just one phenomenon among many." Rather, it's "the phenomenon that *marks* our epoch." But based on Reich's own challenge to the Church (as to whether she is right about the nature of eros as a yearning for God), we can also see how the error of the sexual revolution will end: "It will end by a rediscovery of the full scope of human desire, of its infiniteness,"[24] and by the realization that, contrary to Nietzsche's assertion, God is very much alive.

Recall Edgar Allan Poe's assertion with which this book began: "The origin of poetry lies in a thirst for a wilder Beauty than earth supplies." When man no longer shoots the arrow of his longing beyond this world, the poetry dries up. The vocabulary with which we describe the world then shifts to that of the technician. Thank God for biologists and all they can tell us about the functioning of our bodies. That's fine and good as far as it goes. But thank God also, and all the more so, for poets and mystics and artists who recognize that wilder Beauty and help us enter in! Contrast Wilhelm Reich's reduction of human sexual experience to "bioelectric processes in our tissues" with Victor Hugo's poetic vision of the mystery unfolding on Marius and Cosette's wedding night in *Les Misérables*:

> A little after midnight the . . . house became a temple. . . .
> Upon the threshold of wedding-nights stands an angel smiling.

---

24 Carlo Lancellotti, "'Ideological Colonization': The Global Imposition of Liberal Anthropology," lecture available at https://vimeo.com/412983671.

. . . The soul enters into contemplation before this sanctuary, in which is held the celebration of love. . . . It is impossible that this sacred festival of destiny should not send a celestial radiation to the infinite. Love is the sublime crucible in which is consummated the fusion of man and woman; the one be-ing, the triple being, the final being, the human trinity springs from it. . . The lover is priest. . . Something of this joy goes to God. . . . A nuptial bed makes a halo in the darkness. . . . That little obscure alcove has for its ceiling the whole heavens. When two mouths, made sacred by love, draw near each other to create, it is impossible that above that ineffable kiss there should not be a thrill in the immense mystery of the stars.[25]

That's a man glimpsing the sacramental and prophetic po-tential of the two becoming one flesh! That's a man glimps-ing sexual union as theophany!

Respect for the Artist

To foster and attain that deeper sensibility, one must approach creation itself as a work of art that will whisper the secrets of the Artist's heart if we seek them with honor and reverence. The scientific method, on the other hand, as Galileo himself put it, began by putting nature "on the rack," extracting from her by experimentation the secrets she would not voluntari-ly reveal.[26] Many of her secrets have indeed been "coughed up," but through a coercion that betrays a loss of respect for the mystery. We are God's "*poiēma*," says Saint Paul (Eph 2:10)—a Greek word for skilled work of art, from which we

---

25 Victor Hugo, *Les Misérables* (Oxford University Press, 1876), 441–42.
26 See Benedict XVI, *The Yes of Jesus Christ*, 18.

get the word "poem." A science-is-all mentality, however, simply doesn't "get" God's poetry, so we lose respect for the mega mystery revealed through the sexual difference as a call to fatherhood and motherhood, and we reduce the body to raw biological material.

Re-spect literally means "to look again." It implies that we've missed something on first glance; we're *looking*, but not *seeing*. When we are blind to God's *poiēma* and only perceptive to the body as something biological, it's like reducing the Mona Lisa to the chemical components of the paint. With technical precision we can wax eloquent about the compounds that make up the various pigments placed on the canvas, but we're oblivious to the fact that these pigments have been masterfully configured by Leonardo da Vinci to tell a story, to reveal the beauty of a woman. When we lose sight of the art, we lose sight of the artist and his intention. In such a world, the *visible* is rendered *invisible* to the point that we can lose all perception of what a woman even is.

There's nothing wrong, of course, with gaining specialized knowledge of the chemistry of paints and pigments. The science of art preservation and restoration, for example, provides a great service in safeguarding artistic treasures against the ravages of time. But the value of any preservationist's knowledge is commensurate with his or her fidelity to the original intention of the artist. Those who understand the artistic value of the Mona Lisa would be horrified if technicians claiming to restore Leonardo's masterpiece used their knowledge of paints and pigments to reconfigure the image of that famous smiling woman into that of a bearded man.

When the universe and all it contains is no longer seen as art, then there is no Artist whose intention we need to respect. There is no story, no plan, no mega mystery to revere. "Nature itself," as John Paul II observed, "from being 'mater' (mother)"—something worthy of honor and respect—"is now reduced to being 'matter,' and is subjected to every kind of manipulation."[27] In turn, if the natural world is not an icon of the divine mystery, then neither is the human body, neither is the sexual difference, neither is marriage and human fertility. In this view, our bodies become completely arbitrary. The physical realm—having nothing it points to, nothing it's meant for, no end, no destiny, nothing to "aim at"—becomes disoriented (and disorienting). But not only dis-oriented, for that implies a proper orientation. The physical world, especially our own embodiment, becomes un-oriented—having no orientation at all, other than that which we assign to it and to ourselves. What we usually assign to it is our own pleasure, which turns other people into *means* to our pleasure. We'll stick around as long as people bring us pleasure, but we'll abandon them when they don't. In turn, without the Artist, we play the technicians and claim the right to dominate and manipulate the "raw material" of this physical world, including our own bodies, in any way that promises to please us.

Jean-Paul Sartre summed up this view quite well when he asserted that "there is no human nature because there is no God to conceive of it. Man," he concluded, "is nothing other than what he makes of himself."[28] At this point Descartes's dictum, "I think therefore I am," has logically proceeded to: "I think therefore I am whatever I think I am."

---

27 John Paul II, *Evangelium Vitae* 22.
28 Jean-Paul Sartre, *Existentialism Is a Humanism* (Yale University Press, 2007), 22.

Having embraced this new Cartesian Gnosticism with gusto, the secular world today promotes *an infinite number of "gender identities" and erotic orientations.* The Church, on the other hand, wishing to honor the Artist and the meaning of his beautiful *poiēma,* discerns in the integrity of our *God-given identity*—"male and female he created them" (Gen 1:27)—that *eros is oriented toward the Infinite.* The former is evidence that we've lost the divine sense of humor and made peace with the confusion caused by the blurry, flat, colorless movie in which we now find ourselves immersed in this fallen world. The latter is a clarion call to listen to the "echo" that remains in the human heart of the original music and color and vibrancy of our true story. The former is evidence that the "enlightenment" of our bodies has become darkness. The latter is a clarion call to bring our bodies whole and entire into the divine light, so that no part of them remains in darkness (see Lk 11:36). It is a clarion call to refuse to normalize the confusion of a fallen world and instead to look for the rays of beauty-as-theophany that still break through, placing all hope in what they promise: the cry of our hearts will not go unanswered; we are made for the Infinite bliss of the Trinitarian Communion, and our creation as male and female is the divine poetry that foreshadows this beautiful destiny awaiting us on the other side.

"It is this immortal instinct for beauty," asserts the French poet Charles Baudelaire, "that thrusts us to regard the world and all its splendors as a reverberation, a resonance of heaven."[29] Letting this heavenly reverberation reverberate through us is what it means to laugh with the sacramentality of the

29 Charles Baudelaire, *Art Romantique, XI: "Notes nouvelles sur Edgar Poe III," IV.*

world. This also, as we will learn in the following chapters, is what it means to live and experience the Church's liturgy in its fullness.

INTO THE MYSTIC

1. What's something you learned in this chapter that you hadn't known before?

2. Have you understood that the *one* aim, the *one* goal, the *one* purpose for which the Catholic Church exists is to lead the world into the ecstasy of eternal nuptials? If you have not, what have you understood the Catholic Church to be? Who has given you a mistaken impression of the Church's purpose and mission? Can you ask God for the grace to forgive those people?

3. Which image of the Christian faith is closer to your experience of it: a call out of darkness that leads to being *seized by Beauty* and *enraptured by God's "mad eros"*; or a lifeless acceptance of cold, dry doctrines and the imposition of seemingly arbitrary rules that appear to rob us of the very zest of life and all hope of fulfilling our deepest desires? If neither of these capture your experience, what does?

4. In what ways have you been treated with lack of re-spect as God's *poiēma*? In what ways have you failed to show others such re-spect? Are you able now to put those painful memories in the light and allow God's merciful love to begin the process of healing?

CHAPTER 6

Idolize, Despise, or Liturgize

The hour is coming when true worshipers will worship the Father in Spirit and in truth.

—JESUS (JN 4:23)

Worship is derived from "worth-ship." We all worship something, which is to say we all ascribe *ultimate worth* to one thing or another. And that to which we ascribe ultimate worth, that which has ultimate value in our lives, is typically whatever we think will satisfy our deepest hunger and thirst. In other words, we worship whatever we think will quench eros.

We must be careful to recognize that "quench" can have two very different meanings: to fulfill or to extinguish. When the psalmist says, "The Lord is my shepherd there is nothing I shall want" (23:1), he's speaking a prophecy of *fulfilled* desire, not *extinguished* desire. When we confuse holiness with the latter, we may well end up worshiping what we suppose to be our own "righteousness" gained by willfully suffocating our passions and externally "playing the saint."

When our goal is the fulfillment of eros, we'll either worship God as that fulfillment: "O God, you are my God—it is you I seek! For you my body yearns, for you my soul thirsts, like a dry land without water" (Ps 63:2); or, we'll turn to a great multitude of God-substitutes: typically sensual pleasures, power, prestige, and/or wealth.

Whatever we may worship—be it God, earthly pleasures, or our own apparent "righteousness"—it is inextricably linked with our approach to eros. Furthermore, since eros is inextricably linked with human sexuality, worship is likewise inextricably linked with our embodiment as male and female. Saint Paul makes this particularly clear in his letter to the Romans, both with regard to false worship, in which we "present the parts of [our] bodies to sin as weapons for wickedness," and with regard to true worship, in which we "present the parts of [our] bodies to God as weapons for righteousness" (Rom 6:13). True or false worship, in turn, orients our whole lives toward two opposite destinies. For when we present "the parts of [our] bodies as slaves to impurity," its "end is death." But when we "present them as slaves to righteousness . . . its end is eternal life" (Rom 6:19–22). "I urge you therefore, brothers, by the mercies of God, to offer your bodies as a living sacrifice, holy and pleasing to God." To do so, Saint Paul affirms, is true "spiritual worship" (Rom 12:1).

I wish to unfold in this chapter the three basic choices we have with our erotically charged embodiment as male and female: we will either *idolize* it, *despise* it, or *liturgize* it.[1] Christian liturgy has one goal: to teach us *true worship*.

---

1   My book *Fill These Hearts: God, Sex, & the Universal Longing* is dedicated

In other words, the goal of liturgy is to orient eros toward that which truly satisfies: bodily participation as male and female in the eternal ecstasy of the Trinitarian exchange via the marriage between Christ, the Bridegroom, and the Church, his Bride. If we don't learn this way of true worship, there's only one other option: false worship—which is to say, if we're not learning the way of *liturgizing* our sexed bodies (that is, our bodies as male and female), we are doomed as a culture to flip-flop between *idolizing* and *despising* them. We're tempted to *idolize* them whenever we think they can satisfy the cry of eros. Then, as we mentioned in the previous chapter, we eventually *despise* them for failing to deliver on the promise we invested in them.[2]

Idolizing Our Sexed Bodies

Idolatry "remains a constant temptation to faith," the *Catechism* tells us.[3] Why? It seems to have something to do with the very nature of sacramentality and theophany. As we've been discussing from the start, God created all the beauties and sensual pleasures of this earth as so many icons of his eternal Beauty. In a very real way, sensual pleasures

to unfolding these three choices at some length. There I describe these choices with the metaphor of fast-food, starvation, and banquet. Taking our hunger to the fast-food puts us on the path of the *addict*; starving ourselves puts us on the path of the *stoic*; while opening our hunger to the divine banquet puts us on the path of the *mystic*.

2   The "we" here indicates the culture at large and over a span of time. Given enough life experience, our individual lives may reflect the same pattern as the culture, but it's also frequent that a person grows up in an atmosphere of despising the body without any personal experience of having idolized it first. Or one may grow up in an atmosphere of idolizing the body without any personal experience of having despised it first. Very few, tragically, grow up in an atmosphere of liturgizing the body.

3   CCC 2113.

(the pleasures we experience through our senses) are meant to provide a foretaste of heaven, a small glimmer of God's extravagant goodness and joy, in which we're invited to participate eternally. But precisely because these icons can provide a *taste* of heaven, there is a "constant temptation" to treat them *as* heaven—that is, to idolize them.

Again, in his Letter to the Romans, Saint Paul describes how we descend into the desecration of eros and the idolization of our sexed bodies.[4] First Paul speaks of the revelation of divine Beauty through created beauty (theophany): "Ever since the creation of the world, his invisible attributes of eternal power and divinity have been able to be understood and perceived in what he has made" (Rom 1:20). The proper human response to theophany is to entrust oneself to it wholeheartedly, allowing eros to carry us aloft in praise of and thanksgiving to God for the taste of heaven he has granted, and to celebrate joyfully the hope this theophany has inspired of one day passing over into an eternal participation in Beauty itself. *That's* liturgy. As Saint Augustine says: "If you find pleasure in bodily things, praise God for them, and direct your love to their maker."[5]

If we fail to *liturgize*—that is, if we fail to allow the eros that's been awakened in us by theophany to take flight and pass over from beauty to Beauty—our hearts will mistake that which aroused eros (the creature) for that which alone can satisfy it (the Creator). *That's* idolatry. Saint Paul speaks of it plainly as the next step in the sequence: "Although they knew God [via theophany], they did not accord him glory

---

4   The main insights in what follows regarding this sequence in Romans 1 are adapted from Dr. Timothy Patitsas. See "Chastity and Empathy," 40–41.

5   Saint Augustine, *Confessions* 4:12.

as God or give him thanks [for his theophany]. Instead . . . their senseless minds were darkened [blinded to the Beauty to which beauty points]. While claiming to be wise, they became fools and exchanged the glory of the immortal God for the likeness of an image of mortal man" (Rom 1:21–23).

Here Paul is repeating an insight from the book of Wisdom on the nature of idolatry: "Foolish by nature were all who . . . from studying the works did not discern the artisan. Instead . . . they considered gods [the things God had made]. Now if out of joy in their beauty they thought them gods, let them know how far more excellent is the Lord than these; for the original source of beauty fashioned them. For from the greatness and the beauty of created things their original Author, by analogy, is seen." Such idolaters "have gone astray," as the author of Wisdom acknowledges, "though they seek God and wish to find him. For they search busily among his works, but are distracted by what they see, because the things seen are fair" (Wis 13:1–7).

When beauty distracts us from Beauty, the heart gets "stuck" on the symbol of that for which it yearns and fixates on finite sensual pleasures as if they were able to quench the yearning of eros for infinite joy. That's what sexual lust is in its very essence: a grasping at and domination of another's beauty for the sake of one's own selfish gratification. Having turned a blind eye to the theophany that reveals God's gen-*eros*-ity, lust is a thankless affair, which is to say it's noneucharistic/nonliturgical, or even antieucharistic/ antiliturgical: "they did not accord him glory as God or give him thanks" (Rom 1:21). Why? Because they "exchanged the truth of God for a lie," as Paul says (Rom 1:25)—the lie that God does not want to satisfy eros!

"*There is only one temptation,*" says Albacete. "All particular temptations are expressions of this one original or 'primordial' temptation. It is the temptation to believe that the fulfillment of the desires of the human heart depends entirely on us."[6] Saint John Paul II called this the doubting of the gift.[7] Through the acceptance of the lie, we came to doubt and ultimately deny that our heavenly Father was a giver of good gifts; we came to doubt and deny that the Infinite One wanted to fulfill our yearning: "Take your delight in the Lord and he will grant you the desire of your heart" (Ps 37:4). But even when we deny the gift, the thirst for the Infinite does not disappear. Instead, as Benedict XVI put it, we begin a desperate and sterile search for "false infinites."[8] In turn, we grasp at whatever semblance of satisfaction sensual pleasures provides for our beleaguered souls, and guard with our very lives the "right" to do so because we mistakenly think *that's all there is.* Tragically, at this point, for lack of faith that beauty leads to Beauty (and that that Beauty is "gift" to us) "the good things that God has created as paths that lead to him become idols that replace the Creator."[9]

Why is the world's main idol so often the beauty of the body and the allure of sex? Because in the divine plan the beauty of the sexual difference and the call of the two to become "one flesh" is the main icon in the created order of the divine mystery (see Gen 1:27–28; Eph 5:31–32). Which brings us to the final step in Saint Paul's sequence: it is precisely

---

6 Lorenzo Albacete, *Magnificat*, Holy Week, 2010, 124.
7 See John Paul II, TOB 26:4.
8 Benedict XVI, Letter addressing the *Communion and Liberation* gathering in Rimini, Italy, August 10, 2012.
9 Ibid.

because of the idolatry of our sexed bodies that "God handed them over to impurity through the lusts of their hearts for the mutual degradation of their bodies" (Rom 1:24). The word we want to explore next is "degradation." As history plainly demonstrates, when a culture fails to respect the mega *mystery* of our creation as male and female, eventually we experience our sexed bodies as a mega *misery*, which is to say: a culture will eventually *despise* whatever it has *idolized* (precisely what is meant to be *liturgized*).

Despising Our Sexed Bodies

In preparation for her documentary film *Embrace*, which explores the issue of body loathing, Taryn Brumfitt asked one hundred women to use one word that described their bodies. "Disgusting," "gross," and other similarly negative words were a tragically constant refrain. Her film reports that 91 percent of women express some form of hatred or rejection of their bodies.

If this is how you feel about your body, there's no need to worry. There are plenty of enterprising business ventures ready and willing both to foster and then capitalize on your poor body image, such as the plastic surgery practice whose billboard for liposuction proclaims: "We suck so you don't have to!"[10] This sums up well the sentiment of a culture that idolizes the human body on the one hand while fomenting a culture of people who despise their bodies on the other. And it's not just a problem affecting women. Male cosmetic surgeries have increased 325 percent since 1997. And balding

---

10   This was a billboard I saw with my own eyes driving into New York City some years ago.

men have made the hair-replacement industry worth an estimated $1.5 billion.[11]

We are constantly told by the media that we are too fat or too thin; too short or too tall; too flabby or too wrinkled; too hairy or not hairy enough. We are constantly told that our eyes, skin, or hair are the wrong color; that our faces are too blotchy or our complexions are not smooth enough; various body parts should be bigger or smaller, rounder or flatter, firmer or softer. In short, we are constantly told to scrutinize virtually every aspect of our anatomy, and because of the photoshopped ideals exalted by our culture, we inevitably find our own bodies wanting.

The problem of body loathing goes far deeper, however, than lamenting that we don't measure up to society's ideal image of physical beauty. As the furor over "identity politics" makes clear, we've gotten to the point of raging against the sexual difference itself. Indeed, we've become a culture at war with the very idea of "male and female he created them" (Gen 1:27). As radical feminist author Shulamith Firestone made plain at the very start of the feminist revolution, the end goal of the revolution she espoused must be "the elimination of . . . the sex *distinction* itself [so that] genital differences between human beings would no longer matter culturally."[12]

What makes genital differences matter? Precisely their ability in union with each other to generate new life. That Greek root "gen" means "to produce or give birth to." Beyond the

---

11   Raj Chander, "With Superheroes Comes the Pressure of Unrealistic Male Bodies," Healthline.com, updated October 18, 2018, https://www.healthline.com/health/mental-health/male-body-image-problems#4.

12   Shulamith Firestone, *The Dialectic of Sex* (William Morrow and Co., 1970), 11.

words "genitals" and "generate," we see it in words like "genesis," "generous," "progeny," "genealogy," and, yes, "gender." Prior to its modern rupture from the body, the word "gender" always referred to "the manner in which one *generates* new life." And that, of course, is determined by that other "gen" word we're discussing: our *genitals*. The male gender's genitals generate the next generation with sperm. The female gender's genitals generate the next generation with ova. Furthermore, by genetic design, males generate new life within another, while females generate new life within themselves. Women alone get pregnant, but they don't get pregnant alone. Hence, if the modern agenda to eliminate the cultural significance of genital difference were to succeed, it would need to turn women into the kind of beings that can engage in genital intercourse without getting pregnant—the kind of beings otherwise known as *men*.

Thus enters the modern mandate for readily available and effective contraception. In turn, to keep the illusion going that men and women are "the same," when efforts to sterilize the womb fail, people demand the "right" to destroy the evidence. Thus enters the modern mandate for unrestricted access to abortion. It takes some time due to what sociologist William Ogburn called "cultural lag,"[13] but introduce contraception and abortion on a wide scale and eventually the fundamental link between gender, genitals, and generating— which has always shaped civilization at its very foundations— will vanish almost entirely from the way we understand our personal relationships and our personal identities. *That's* the

---

13 See Mark Regnerus, *Cheap Sex: The Transformation of Men, Marriage, and Monogamy* (Oxford University Press, 2017), 146–48.

world the revolutionaries envisioned, and it is, indeed, upon us. Not wanting to concede, however, that the vanishing of the sex distinction also entails the vanishing of humanity's future, the agenda Firestone outlined anticipated a world in which pregnancy was replaced by artificial reproduction (mechanical wombs perhaps?) through which the "tyranny of the biological family would be broken."[14]

Notice that human fertility (the fact that sex leads to babies), and female fertility in particular (the fact that women conceive and carry them), is here considered as some form of cosmic oppression. Rather than seeing in woman's womb an evocative symbolism revealing the divine gen-*eros*-ity, radical feminism sees woman's capacity to become a mother as a "biological tyrant" that must be overthrown—as something to erase rather than embrace; as something to eliminate rather than celebrate. Translation: the rejection of what a woman actually *is* (the kind of being who can get pregnant through genital intercourse) is now considered essential to the promotion of women. In turn, those who love and want to honor what a woman actually *is* (the kind of being who can get pregnant through genital intercourse) are accused of hating women. How did the world become so convoluted that what is in fact misogyny is now called "love for women," and what is in fact love for women is now called "misogyny"?

For those with eyes to see, there is no doubt that behind all this confusion "lurks a seductive voice, opposed to God, which makes [us] fall into death out of envy."[15] Right from the beginning, the "father of lies" wanted to replace the

14 Firestone, *The Dialectic of Sex*, 11.
15 CCC 391.

truth of God's gen-*eros*-ity (revealed through our bodies as male and female) with the lie that God is a tyrant whose rule must be overthrown. Notice that from the beginning to the end of the biblical drama the enemy is after "the woman" and her ability to bear offspring (see Gen 3:15 and Rev 12:4). Why? Because he's an excarnating anti-Christ from the beginning and the *Logos* takes flesh through her. It's a bedrock principle of biblical faith: God comes to us *through woman*, more specifically, *through her fertile womb*. If there's an enemy who wants to thwart this divine plan, it makes sense that he'd aim all his diabolic fury *right there*. Indeed, he has always wanted to "devour the child"[16] (Rev 12:4).

If, as we observed in the previous chapter, a woman's womb is a witness to heaven and a man's testicles are a testimony to the eternal Fatherhood of God, then it makes sense that the enemy despises our sexed bodies and, out of envy, wants us to despise them, too. Contraception and abortion manifest a diabolical despising of the genital function. They demonstrate a specific determination to activate our generative *energy* while at the same time refusing all *synergy* with the Lord and giver of life. *That* is what the enemy wants: he wants to rupture all synergy, all communion, between the Creator and the creature. Because the gender distinction with its inherent call to generate the next generation represents the fundamental call to synergy and communion

---

16 This is precisely what is happening in abortion clinics around the world. I say this not to shame those who in desperation may resort to procuring an abortion, but to turn the lights on so we can see what is happening in our world today. Satan has always wanted to turn the womb into a tomb, and look how successful he's been. But Christ defeats him by turning the tomb back into a womb!

with the God who *is* Eternal Generation, *that's* what the enemy attacks. His goal is to get us to render our genitals unable to generate in order to blind us to the meaning of gender. By doing so he thus eclipses the theophany of our bodies, which reveals the Covenant Love of the God who wants to marry us so that we might conceive eternal life within us.[17]

Recall John Paul II's words: "Each and every time that *motherhood* is repeated in human history, it is always *related to the Covenant* which God established with the human race through the motherhood of the Mother of God."[18] Once again we are face-to-face with why the enemy hates motherhood and matri-mony (which means "the call to motherhood"). "Is not the Bible trying to tell us that it is precisely in the 'woman' . . . that history witnesses a dramatic struggle for every human being, the struggle for his or her fundamental 'yes' or 'no' to God and his eternal plan for humanity?"[19] In Mary's unreserved "yes" to conceiving and carrying the Son of God in her womb, "the Gift of God found the acceptance he had awaited from the beginning of time."[20] As Joseph Ratzinger observed:

> Mary thus represents saved and liberated man, but she does so precisely as a woman. . . . The "biological" and the human are inseparable in the figure of Mary, just as are the human and the "theological." This insight [contradicts] the

---

17 For a more detailed exploration of this idea (and for how this attack was predicted by the Blessed Mother in her appearances in Fatima in 1917), see my book *Eclipse of the Body: How We Lost the Meaning of Sex, Gender, Marriage, and the Family and How to Regain It* (Totus Tuus Press, 2018).

18 John Paul II, *Mulieris Dignitatem* 19.

19 Ibid., 30.

20 CCC 2617.

dominant movements of our time . . . at the very core. For
. . . today's anthropological program hinges more radically
than ever before on . . . a detachment of man from his biological conditionality, from the "male and female he created
them" [of the divine plan]. This sexual difference is something that man, as a biological being, can never get rid of,
something that marks man in the deepest center of his being.
Yet [today] it is regarded as a totally irrelevant triviality, as a
constraint arising from historically fabricated "roles," and is
therefore consigned to the "purely biological realm," which
[they say] has nothing to do with man as such. Accordingly,
this "purely biological" dimension is treated as a thing that
man can manipulate at will to be simply a "human being"
who is neither male nor female. But in reality man thereby
strikes a blow against his deepest being. He holds himself in
contempt, because the truth is that he is human only insofar
as he is bodily, only insofar as he is man or woman. When
man reduces this fundamental determination of his being to
a despicable trifle that can be treated as a thing, he himself
becomes a trifle and a thing, and his "liberation" turns out
to be his degradation. Whenever biology is subtracted from
humanity, humanity itself is negated. Thus, the question of
the legitimacy of maleness as such and of femaleness as such
has high stakes: nothing less than the reality of the creature.
Since the biological determinateness of humanity is least possible to hide in motherhood, an emancipation that negates
bios [biology] is a particular aggression against the woman. It
is the denial of her right to be a woman. Conversely, the preservation of creation is in this respect bound up in a special
way with the question of woman. And the Woman in whom
the "biological" is "theological"—that is, motherhood of

God—is in a special way the point where the paths [of man's (and all of creation's) true and false liberation] diverge.[21]

A culture that claims contraception and abortion as fundamental "rights" is a culture seeking liberation from the natural consequences of sex so that people can indulge their sexual compulsions unencumbered by children and the responsibility of lovingly raising them. If we take a deeper look, we'll realize that such "liberation" is a smokescreen for bondage to libido. Authentic sexual liberation is not the liberty to indulge one's compulsions; it's *liberation from the compulsion to indulge.* Only such a person is free to be a gift to another without degrading the other into an object of gratification. Far from cancelling out or negating the powers and passions of eros, such liberation channels those powers and passions toward loving, self-sacrificial behavior for the good of both the current generation and of the next. As intense as the passion of lust can be, the passion of love is far more intense; it's a "vehement flame, the flame of the Lord" that "rivers cannot extinguish" (Song 8:6–7).

While false sexual liberation begins with an unflinching determination to sever genitals from their generating power, authentic sexual liberation begins with an unflinching determination to reverence that power. Lack of reverence for the fact that genitals lead to generation can only lead to degeneration.[22] By allowing us to skirt responsibility for channeling

---

21 Ratzinger, *Mary: The Church at the Source*, 31–33.

22 At the source of all life is love: life-giving love. This is the foundation of the universe and of every human life. It's also the parable, the theophany, written into the natural world, culminating in human sexual difference. Follow that logic and everything the Catholic Church teaches about sex

eros toward the true, the good, and the beautiful, contraception and abortion unleash the false, the bad, and the ugly. When we intentionally render the sexual act sterile, the goal of sex shifts from establishing lasting family bonds (recall the Latin root of religion is *religare*, "to form a bond") to experiencing fleeting selfish pleasures.[23] In this kind of sexual economy, you're "valued" if you bring such pleasures, and you're discarded if you do not. Either way, it leads to the "degrading of our bodies," which Saint Paul spoke of in Romans 1. Indeed, today we are freefalling into an abyss of ever more hellish bodily degradations.

Because we are body-persons, the degrading of our bodies is always the degrading of our-*selves*. Eventually the interior wound to the person becomes so acute that it must be expressed (pressed out) in one way or another. We see this in the compulsively inflicted harm of various eating disorders. We see it in the grotesque forms of tattoos, body piercings, and gauging that are becoming commonplace.[24] We see it in

and gender and marriage will make perfect, beautiful sense. We can rail against it all we like, but in the end, it's embracing or rejecting that incarnate parable that determines whether we flourish or flounder, whether we return to our source or reject it.

23 Reverence for the fact that genitals lead to generation does not mean couples are without recourse if a just reason arises to avoid a pregnancy. In such a situation, reverence for the power of genitals to generate leads a couple to refrain from genital intercourse during the fertile phase of a woman's cycle. When properly trained in modern methods of Natural Family Planning, this can be determined with 98–99 percent accuracy. When people ask me what the moral difference is between sterilizing the act yourself and just waiting until it's naturally infertile, I ask them what the moral difference is between killing Grandma and just waiting until she dies naturally. In one, God remains God. In the other, we take the powers of life into our own hands and make ourselves like God. Learn more in my book *Good News about Sex & Marriage: Answers to Your Honest Questions about Catholic Teaching* (TOBI Press).

24 Gauging is the practice of inserting larger and larger "gauges" into one's

intentional cutting and scarring and in the mainstreaming of sadomasochism. We see it in the direct killing (and often dismemberment) of innocent human life in the womb. And we see it in the cultural endorsement of the mutilation of healthy, functioning breasts and genitals in "transgender surgeries."[25] These are all outward signs ("sacraments," if you will) of the *horrific interior pain* we are in as a culture because we've lost sight of the theophany of our bodies.

Can we not recognize that this collective "primal scream" is part of the whole creation groaning for the redemption of the body (see Rom 8:18–23)? Timothy Patitsas suggests that such manifestations of our pain indicate a kind of "proto-repentance" going up to heaven that is honest and direct.[26] The pain of not knowing our true and splendorous identity as sexual-body-persons will be answered with superabundant mercy for all who join in the "loud cry" of Christ from the Cross (see Mk 15:37). Speaking of this cry, the *Catechism* says: "All the troubles, for all time, of humanity enslaved by

---

earlobes, lips, or other fleshy parts of the body, creating disfigured loops of stretched flesh.

25 Abigail Favale insightfully observes: "Because bodily sex has been divorced from procreative potential, reduced to appearance and pleasure-making, the prospect of changing one's sex has become feasible. If 'man' and 'woman' are defined in terms of generative potentiality, it is simply impossible to change sex. A scalpel can sterilize; it can permanently impede procreative potential, but a scalpel cannot endow the procreative potential of the other sex. Elaborate surgical and hormonal interventions can alter the appearance of the body and mimic sex markers—and that is enough for us now, because that is what bodily sex has become. A surgeon can make a vagina out of a wound, because the vagina is no longer seen as the door to a womb" ("The Eclipse of Sex by the Rise of Gender," *Church Life Journal*, March 1, 2019, https://churchlifejournal.nd.edu/articles/the-eclipse-of-sex-by-the-rise-of-gender/).

26 See Patitsas, "Chastity and Empathy," 35.

sin and death, all the petitions and intercessions of salvation history are summed up in this cry of the incarnate Word. Here the Father accepts them and, beyond all hope, answers them by raising his Son."[27]

Without hope in the salvific power of Christ's death and Resurrection, however, we take matters into our own hands. With the false promise of escaping the pain that despising the body causes, we (understandably) opt for a schizophrenic rupture of the "self" from the body, which, in turn, allows us to justify harming and disfiguring our bodies in the name of defending our excarnate "selves." But this approach, as we have seen, is quite literally *diabolic*: it ruptures the God-ordained marriage of body and soul. We must witness once again to the *symbolic* meaning of the body, to the fact that our bodies are *meant* for the Lord and that Christ is "the savior of the body" (Eph 5:23)! This means that *any-body* who has ever felt like *no-body* can reclaim the full truth that he or she is *some-body*, and this hope is for *every-body*! This redemption of our bodies is precisely the hope we encounter and are invited to enter into through the Church's liturgy.

Liturgizing Our Sexed Bodies

Whether we tend toward idolizing or despising our sexed bodies, both are a sure sign that we have lost sensitivity to theophany. Albacete used to insist that one of the best antidotes to this loss is good art. Art expresses the language of the heart and has the power to awaken our deepest passions. Good art helps us direct those passions toward all that is true, good, and beautiful, even enabling us to pass over in some

---

27 CCC 2606.

way from beauty to Beauty. Bad art does the opposite, funneling our passions toward false infinities. In other words, good art consecrates eros, while bad art desecrates it; good art liturgizes eros, while bad art bastardizes it.

Our culture is awash in this kind of bad art. Human beings are not the same thing as the images that flash across our screens. We are much more because of our vocation to love, which introduces us as male and female into the realm of the "mega mystery."[28] In the absence of any sense of this mega mystery, the modern world has promoted the satisfaction of eros through an idolatrous quest for the "perfectly beautiful body," which has led precisely to the despising of the body that we outlined above. While the destructiveness of this idolatry must be called out, we must also be careful here not to throw out the baby with the bathwater. Our tendency to worship beautiful bodies is not altogether wrong, for perfect Beauty has taken flesh, making the Body of Christ "the focal point of all worship."[29]

In a retreat given to artists in 1962, the future Pope John Paul II reflected as follows on a profound experience he had when he encountered the ancient Greek portrayal of the idealized human body:

I'm reminded of the day when I wandered for many hours around the Baths of Diocletian in Rome. I encountered the masterpieces of ancient Greek sculpture there. That was a very laborious day. I took great pains and noticed with what immense effort all those people, those great masters of

28 See John Paul II, *Letter to Families* 20.
29 Benedict XVI, *A New Song for the Lord: Faith in Christ and Liturgy Today* (Crossroad Publishing, 1996), 153.

sculpture, had sought to demonstrate perfect, absolute beauty in the human body, and in doing so they had been seeking the Incarnation. After this walk of many hours—it took such a great effort to spend time with that ancient pagan art—I understood the Gospel anew. And I understood it better. I understood that what had been the subject of the search for absolute, impeccably perfect beauty in the human body—that was the Beauty which did indeed become incarnate in the Gospel: God who became Man; God who revealed himself, because he appeared in the flesh. Together with his presence, he brought with him an entire special world of Beauty. Beauty that is peculiar to himself; Beauty which is identical with him, just as he is identical with Beauty.[30]

Notice the painstaking efforts he made to understand what the human heart is really desiring in its pursuit of idealized bodies: it's looking for Ultimate Beauty in the flesh. In other words, the human heart, whether we know it or not, is looking for the incarnate *Logos*. When false worship runs its course and leaves the heart yearning still (think of the prodigal son having gorged on the pleasures of the world and finding himself still hungry), the heart is all the more prepared to discover true worship as the reorientation of eros toward that which truly satisfies (think of the prodigal son returning to the Father's house). This is what it means to liturgize our erotically charged embodiment as male and female.

Nowhere is this understanding of true worship more explicit than in the encounter between Jesus and the woman at

---

30 Karol Wojtyla, *God Is Beauty: A Retreat on the Gospel and Art* (TOBI Press), 24–25.

the well. Venerated by the Eastern Church as Saint Photine (meaning "luminous one"), the Samaritan woman represents the journey everyone must undertake from *idolizing* and/or *despising* the body-sex-eros, to *liturgizing* them, opening and entrusting one's deepest thirst to the One who alone can quench it. Indeed, we can recognize a model of the liturgy itself in the way Saint John the Evangelist unfolds Photine's story.

Liturgy is the setting where God's marital Covenant with humanity is both proposed and enacted. For those familiar with the Old Testament, the setting of Jesus's encounter with this woman—Jacob's well—also conjures up the remembrance of various important wedding proposals.[31] Christ comes to the well thirsting for his Bride, just as he does in the liturgy. The Samaritans, Israelites who had intermarried with foreigners, represented those who had adulterated themselves with false worship: "they have forsaken me, the source of living waters; they have dug themselves . . . broken cisterns that cannot hold water" (Jer 2:13). Photine, having taken her thirst to many broken cisterns, now comes to Jacob's well with her thirst, just as we must come to the liturgy with ours. And she meets a mysterious Jewish man who, breaking all custom and sense of propriety, first presents his thirst to her, saying, "Give me a drink" (Jn 4:7).

The *Catechism* describes the liturgy when it proclaims that "God's initiative of love always comes first; our own first step is always a response." Indeed the "wonder of prayer is revealed beside the well where we come seeking water: there, Christ comes to meet every human being. It is he who first seeks us and asks us for a drink. Jesus thirsts; his asking arises

---

31   For examples, see Genesis 24, 29, and Exodus 2.

from the depths of God's desire for us. Whether we realize it or not, prayer is the encounter of God's thirst with ours. God thirsts that we may thirst for him."[32] *That* is what it means to liturgize eros. It means to turn it into prayer: "The Fathers of the Church say that prayer, properly understood, is nothing other than becoming a longing for God."[33] To be a saint is nothing other than to become an all-consuming eros for the living God, and if we let the liturgy have its way with us, that indeed is what we shall become.

We must let Jesus speak to us intimately in the liturgy of the Word, just as he did with Photine. If we listen attentively to the prayers and readings, he will tell us everything we ever did (see Jn 4:29)—not in order to condemn us; rather, in order to redirect our desire toward what we really desire. In other words, he will gently show us our false worship (our idols) in order to lead us to true worship. Jesus's words, "Go call your husband," indicate the direction in which Photine had been aiming her heart's thirst and her body's longing. Having been married five times and now living with a man to whom she was not married (see Jn 4:18), Photine had had six lovers. Six, of course, is the imperfect biblical number. Jesus comes to her as her "seventh lover," the perfect biblical number. Jesus thus presents himself to the Samaritan woman (who, let us recall, symbolizes adulterous Israel and, thus, all of us) as her perfect satisfaction.

Notice how gentle Jesus is in redirecting her desire: "If you knew the gift of God and who is saying to you, 'Give me a drink,' you would have asked him and he would have given you living water" (Jn 4:10). It's as if he were saying: "I know

---

32   CCC 2567, 2560.
33   Joseph Ratzinger, *Mary: The Church at the Source*, 15.

you are thirsty for love, I know. But, my dearly beloved, *I'm the love you've been looking for!* If you only knew the gift that *I* wanted to give you . . . you would ask, and I would give it to you . . . and you would never thirst again. In fact, the water I give will well up in you to eternal life" (see Jn 4:10–14). He doesn't shame her. He doesn't scold her. Rather, he taps the abyss of her heart's yearning until she realizes "the well is deep" (Jn 4:11). Getting in touch with the depth of her eros makes her cry out for what only Jesus can provide: "Sir, give me this water" (Jn 4:15)! In this way, asking for the gift that will satisfy her thirst reverses the "doubting of the gift" in which original sin consists.

Without introducing artificial divisions, we can recognize here a transition to the liturgy of the Eucharist. Leaving our old water jars behind (see Jn 4:28), we bring our thirst to the living water that is Christ poured out from the altar. When we find that which truly satisfies our thirst and vulnerably open ourselves to receive so great a gift, then we are worshiping the Father "in Spirit and in truth" (Jn 4:24). Note the allusion to the Trinity: Father, Spirit, and Truth (Jesus *is* the truth, as he says in John 14:6). To worship the Father in Spirit and Truth is to say to the Trinity with our entire erotically charged body-soul humanity as male or as female: "*To participate in your eternal ecstasy is of ultimate worth and is everything I desire!*" That, according to Saint Augustine, is what Christians mean when they say the word "God." With that word we wish to express "all that we yearn for."[34]

In turn, having found "all that we yearn for," we, like Photine, naturally want to introduce others to Jesus, saying:

---

34 Saint Augustine, Homily on First Letter of John.

"Could he possibly be the Messiah" (Jn 4:29)? And so the liturgy ends with a call to *mission* (from which we get the word "Mass"): "Go and announce the Gospel of the Lord." As we learn from Photine, evangelization is nothing other than one thirsty person telling another thirsty person where to find living water. In and through the announcement of the Gospel of the Lord, we are inviting others to liturgize their lives, their bodies, their desires. That means we are inviting them to place all that they are—all their concerns, fears, misdirected desires, sins, hopes, idols, trials, sorrows, problems—on the altar where they can be "transubstantiated" (changed in substance) into something Beautiful.

This is the extraordinary power and gift of liturgy. As Benedict XVI affirms, on the Cross Christ transformed all suffering and all that is wrong with the world "into 'thanks' and therefore into 'blessing.' Hence, he fundamentally transubstantiated life and the world, and he has given us and gives us each day the bread of true life, which transcends this world thanks to the strength of his love." In the liturgy "we wish to insert ourselves into the 'thanks' of the Lord, and thus truly receive the newness of life and contribute to the 'transubstantiation' of the world so that it might not be a place of death, but of life: a world in which love has conquered death."[35]

Liturgy places us within Christ's victory over death—a concrete, *bodily* victory: "Whoever eats my flesh and drinks my blood has eternal life, and I will raise him on the last day" (Jn 6:54). If this bodily victory over death is real, we needn't

---

35 Benedict XVI, Statement on the 65th anniversary of his ordination, June 28, 2016.

anxiously suck into our bodies whatever finite pleasures this world may have to offer us; and we needn't blame our bodies when they fail to satisfy the demands of eros, nor for the inevitable prospect of suffering and death. The flip-flopping we do (both as individuals and as a culture) between idolizing and despising our sexed bodies is the symptom of a hopeless self-reliance that can—and must—give way to relying on the Infinite gift granted us in the liturgy.

Here, in the liturgy, we are granted the privilege of journeying through the veil from the sign to the reality signified, and thus participating even here and now, through faith, in the everlasting Beauty for which we pine. In and through the liturgy, "we are no longer onlookers at a theophany, but are ourselves enveloped in the cloud."[36] Faith is the entryway. As the *Catechism* says, faith allows us to "taste in advance the light of the beatific vision, the goal of our journey here below. . . . When we contemplate the blessings of faith even now . . . it is as if we already possessed the wonderful things which our faith assures us we shall one day enjoy."[37] This is what makes participating in the liturgy with faith a true taste of heaven on earth.

INTO THE MYSTIC

1. What's something you learned in this chapter that you hadn't known before?

2. To what do you ascribe ultimate worth? Where do you expect to find the fulfillment of eros? In other words, what do you worship?

36 Corbon, *The Wellspring of Worship*, 149.
37 CCC 163.

3. In what ways have you idolized your body or other people's bodies? In what ways have you despised your body or
other people's bodies? In what ways can you now liturgize
your body and help others to do the same?

4. Authentic sexual liberation begins with an unflinching
determination to reverence the fact that genitals are meant
to generate new life. In what ways have you been impact-
ed by the false vision of sexual liberation that begins with
severing genitals from their power to generate new life?

CHAPTER 7

The Song at the Base of All Things

**The hills . . . the meadows . . . the valleys . . .
shout for joy, yes, they sing!**

—PSALM 65:13–14

As we've been saying from the start of this book, the beauty of creatures—finite beauty—has the ability to awaken our desire for infinite Beauty, but it cannot possibly satisfy the eros it awakens. Liturgy—properly received, properly entered into, and properly lived out—is the experience of eros taking flight, allowing the creature to pass over from beauty to Beauty, from the sign to the Mystery signified, from the finite to the Infinite, yet without abandoning the created order. For it is precisely *creatures* who make the pass over, taking the created order with them into the divine realm.

During the Eucharistic prayer, the priest invites us to make precisely this pass over when he says, "Lift up your hearts," and the congregation responds, "We lift them up to the Lord." In "a matchlessly brief formula," the *sursum corda* (Latin for "lift up your hearts"), invites "the inner person, the entirety of the self, [to be] lifted up into the height of God, to that height which is God and which in Christ touches the earth, draws it to itself and pulls it up to itself."[1]

Let's try to take that in: in and through the Incarnation, the height of God *descends* to touch the depths of the earth, and then *ascends* along with the earth it has touched, pulling its depths up to that height which is God. Benedict XVI elaborates as follows: God's *descent* through the Incarnation "is only the first part of the movement." The Incarnation "becomes meaningful and definitive" only when the movement is reversed in *ascent,* that is, "only in the cross and Resurrection. From the Cross the Lord draws everything to himself and [in his bodily Resurrection and Ascension he] carries the flesh—that is, humanity, and the entire physical world—into God's eternity."[2] Christ himself puts it this way: "No one has gone up to heaven except the one who has come down from heaven, the Son of Man" (Jn 3:13). It may seem from these words that no one else has access to the heavenly heights, but here's where the unparalleled gift of the Church's liturgy comes into play. Liturgy is the portal through which Christ descends to our level in order, in turn, to raise us, and all of creation, up with him on his joyride into God's eternity.

Experiencing that joyride, you can't help but break into jubilant song, for you are on your way to the superabundant fulfillment of your deepest desires. Eventually you realize that the song you've discovered welling up in your heart has put you in touch with the jubilant music the entire cosmos

---

1   Benedict XVI, *A New Song for the Lord,* 176.
2   Ibid., 153.

has been making since the dawn of creation. John Paul II expresses this poetically as follows:

> And when the song burst out bell-like embraced me,
> I saw how the words discover your hiding place . . .
> When the first song returns, it will rebound
> in deepest echo against all of creation[3]

The "first song" is the joyful noise of praise and thanksgiving echoing in all of creation. Bishop Robert Barron observes that Israel's temple "was covered, inside and out, by symbols of the cosmos, by animals and plants and planets and stars and so on. The idea being that, when Israel gathered for right praise, it was the whole universe being gathered for right praise."[4] The same is true of the Church's liturgy. As Benedict XVI observes, "Not only human beings have a role in the praise of God. Worship is singing in unison with that which all things bespeak."[5] And what all things bespeak, what all of creation sings about, is the eternal love of God-made-flesh in the womb of a woman in order to draw us up into divine ecstasy.

The Word Becomes Music

Through the Incarnation, the Word—the *Logos*/ultimate Meaning—has entered into the physical, and thus, into the realm of our senses. This means that the "senses are not to be discarded." Rather, if we are to take flight and pass over from

---

3   John Paul II, *The Place Within*, 48.
4   Bishop Barron in Conversation with Jordan Peterson, https://www.youtube.com/watch?v=cXllaoNQmZY.
5   Benedict XVI, *A New Song for the Lord*, 141.

beauty to Beauty, our senses must be "expanded to their widest capacity."[6] As they are expanded in this way, we begin to
sense the presence of the *Logos* everywhere. We begin to see,
hear, taste, smell, and touch the divine Meaning in all things,
because it is this Meaning in which all things live and move
and have their being (see Acts 17:28). When this happens,
Pope Benedict XVI says we are being drawn by primordial
forces beyond mere rationality. We are being drawn by "the
attraction of the hidden sound of creation and the uncovering
of the song that lies at the base of things." We are experiencing what he calls the "musification" of the *Logos*, which is part
of the very logic of the Incarnation. He explains:

> Faith becoming music is a part of the process of the Word
> becoming flesh. . . . The Word becoming music is on the one
> hand sensualization, incarnation. . . . But this musification
> is also itself now the site of the shift in the movement: it is
> not only the incarnation of the Word, but at the same time
> the spiritualization of the flesh [which implies and includes
> the spiritualization of the entire material world]. Wood
> and brass turn into tone; the unconscious and the unsolved
> become ordered and meaningful sound. An embodiment
> comes into play that is spiritualization, and a spiritualization
> occurs that is embodiment. The Christian embodiment is
> always simultaneously a spiritualization, and the Christian
> spiritualization is an embodiment into the body of the in-
> carnate Logos.[7]

---

6   Ratzinger, *Spirit of the Liturgy*, 123.
7   Benedict XVI, *A New Song for the Lord*, 154.

The Word becoming music . . . the musification of the Logos . . . faith becoming music—what marvelous, eye-opening (and ear-opening) expressions! This is the gift of musical instruments: that which earth has given and human hands have made render the eternal silence of the *Logos* audible! When wood and brass turn into tone, we are ear-witnesses not only to the musification of ultimate Meaning/*Logos*, but also to the en-meaning-ment (or "logicization") of the sounds buried within creation. Remember that the *descent* "only becomes final, so to speak, at the moment the movement is reversed" in *ascent*. And this "produces a new unity of all reality."[8] This new unity of all reality (universe means everything "turned into one") comes into focus the more we ascend with the *Logos* to the height of God. Here we gain a God's-eye-view of creation. Instead of creation revealing God, theophany gets reversed and God reveals creation.

Father Thomas Dubay explains that from "the natural point of view we come to know God from the vestiges of himself that he has left in the splendor of the visible universe . . . but it remains a knowledge of the infinite through the finite." The more we pass over from beauty to Beauty, the more "the opposite occurs: we know and appreciate creation through the Creator" and we come to experience "a symphonic oneness" in all of creation. Quoting Saint John of the Cross's *Spiritual Canticle*, Dubay explains that each being "gives 'voice to what God is in it,' and all of them together produce a marvelous harmony: 'So creatures will be for the soul a harmonious symphony of sublime music surpassing all concerts and melodies of the world.'"[9]

8   Ibid.
9   Thomas Dubay, *The Fire Within* (Ignatius, 1989), 188–89.

Can we even imagine such sublime music? It's the song of creation's exuberant joy that its depths are being lifted up to the heights of God. Indeed, the astounding gift of music is that it has the ability to span that distance between the earthly/physical realm and the heavenly/spiritual realm, making the earthly heavenly and the heavenly earthly. Have you ever pondered what you're actually hearing when your soul is being enchanted by the melody of a violin? You're hearing hairs from a horse's tail (that's what a high-quality bow is made of) rubbing against dried-out sheep intestines (that's what the strings of a high-quality violin are made of) amplified by a hollowed-out hunk of tree. Or has it ever dawned on you that the beautiful sounds emanating from a guitar or a piano come from the vibration of melted rocks (that's what the steel strings of a guitar and of a piano are made of) also amplified by a piece of tree?

When we play musical instruments, we are drawing out of them the music that is latent "within" wood and brass and steel and horsehair and sheep guts. And in doing so, we are inviting the ascent of the *Logos* that has already descended into them. We are experiencing something that is part of the process of the Word entering the realm of the senses in order to expand them to their widest capacity so we can perceive the divine via the senses. Again, John Paul II's poetry speaks right to the mystery:

with primordial song you have stretched my lungs . . .
a shower of music falling on my strings—
and in this melody You came as Christ[10]

10 John Paul II, *The Place Within*, 186.

In short, those with ears to hear know that when they encounter the beauty of music, they are encountering the presence of the *Logos*, who has entered creation (descent of the divine Word into the physical order) in order to draw creation up with him into the heights of God (ascent of the physical order into the divine Word). And from within those heights, we begin hearing not just the music latent in a small sampling of what God has created (those things that we've turned into instruments), we start hearing the music latent in *everything* God has created. We discover that all of creation is singing the Song of Songs, and that this manifests "a harmonious symphony of sublime music surpassing all concerts and melodies of the world."

How Do You Solve a Problem Like Maria?

Allow me to provide an example from popular culture of someone who lives and rejoices very simply and humanly in this musification of the *Logos* in creation. Think of Maria from the beloved musical *The Sound of Music*. She was exactly right: the hills are, indeed, *"alive with the sound of music / With songs they have song for a thousand years."* And what does Maria want to do when she encounters the enchanting music of the natural world? Her *"heart wants to sing every song it hears."*[11] In other words, Maria wants to enter the cosmic liturgy, she wants to sing in tune and dance in step with the music of all creation.

But have you ever heard the expression *Those who hear not the music think the dancers mad?* This is why so many of the other nuns in Maria's convent are miffed by her—they don't

---

11 "The Sound of Music," from the soundtrack album, *The Sound of Music*, composed by Richard Rogers, lyrics by Oscar Hammerstein (RCA Victor, 1965).

hear the music that Maria hears. In the song "How Do You Solve a Problem Like Maria," they can make no sense out of why she "waltzes on her way to Mass" and why she's always "singing in the abbey."

How *do* you solve a problem like Maria? The answer comes when we hear that song for the second time in the story. It reappears at the start of her nuptial liturgy as she's walking down the aisle to marry Captain von Trapp. Like the bride in the Song of Songs, Maria's "problem" is that she is "sick with love" (Song 2:5). As someone who hears and dances and sings along with the song of all creation, she's a bride yearning for the coming of the Bridegroom, yearning for the Captain of all of creation, *symbolized* (recall the meaning of that word from the end of Chapter 3) by Captain von Trapp.

The Mother Superior understood this well. Upon returning to the convent from her time with the von Trapps, Maria was eager to make her religious vows right away. But when the Mother Superior realized Maria was motivated to do so by fear of her feelings for the captain, she responded to Maria's plea for help with this wise counsel: "Maria, the love of a man and a woman is holy, too. You have a great capacity to love. What you must find out is how God wants you to spend your love. . . . If you love this man it doesn't mean you love God less."

Here the Mother Superior reveals herself to be someone who "laughs with the sacraments," to return to that expression from Fulton Sheen that we learned in Chapter 1. She understands that the good things of this world, like the love of a man and a woman, are not in competition with God (if we experience them as such, it is only because we are inclined to idolize them). Rather, as we've been emphasizing throughout this book, the things of this world are designed by God as so many theophanies, so many signs of his own eternal plan to marry us. In the liturgy, the ability of created things to lead us to the Creator is stretched to its widest capacity. Humble things like oil, water, wine, and bread—"signs so simple that even believers pass them by with indifference"[12]—become portals to the divine via their interaction with our bodies. As John Paul II insists, "Christianity does not reject matter. Rather, bodiliness is considered in all its value in the liturgical act, whereby the human body . . . is united with the Lord Jesus, who himself took a body for the world's salvation."[13]

The mystery of the Eucharist embraces and penetrates the entirety of the material universe. In and through the Eucharist, all of "creation is projected toward divinization, toward the holy wedding feast, toward unification with the Creator himself."[14] And those with eyes to see recognize that God wrote signs of this wedding feast right into the stars.

The Cosmic Dimension of Liturgy

Do you know why the Church has traditionally prayed her liturgy *ad orientem*—toward the east, the land of the rising sun? Liturgy is always a celebration of *East*-er *Sun*-day. We find a key that unlocks the meaning of this cosmic symbolism in Psalm 19: "The sun comes forth like a bridegroom from his chamber to run his course . . . nothing is concealed from its burning heat" (5–7). "Eating the sunrise," then, is precisely the right image of what we do in the liturgy! The Church's tradition of praying *ad orientem* is intended to *orient* the human eros of the Bride (the Church) toward the divine

---

12 Corbon, *The Wellspring of Worship*, 139.
13 John Paul II, *Orientale Lumen* 11.
14 Benedict XVI, Homily for the Mass of Corpus Domini, June 15, 2006.

eros of the Bridegroom (Christ) and set her in procession to meet him at the place of his coming to meet her. As Cardinal Ratzinger explains, "The common turning toward the east was not a 'celebration toward the wall'; it did not mean that the priest 'had his back to the people'." Rather, it was

> a question of priest and people facing in the same direction, knowing that together they were in procession toward the Lord. They did not close themselves into a circle; they did not gaze at one another; but as the pilgrim People of God, they set off for the *Oriens*, for the Christ who comes to meet us. . . . What corresponds with the reality of what is happening [in the Eucharistic liturgy] is . . . the common movement forward, expressed in a common direction for prayer.[15]

Recall that "prayer, properly understood, is nothing other than becoming a longing for God."[16] Praying *ad orientem* acknowledges that all of creation is ordered toward the nuptials of Christ and the Church, which is to say, all of creation is ordered toward the liturgy. Those who laugh with the sacramentality of the world recognize that in every blade, stalk, fern, vine, shrub, and tree stretching up toward the sun; in every lizard sunbathing on a rock; in every evaporating puddle; and in every open flower we find a proclamation of the nature of true worship/liturgy: to orient our heart's yearning (eros) toward the sun, that is, toward Christ the Bridegroom.

What the rest of creation does unwittingly, we can engage our freedom to do wittingly. This is the distinctive

---

15 Ratzinger, *Spirit of the Liturgy*, 80, 81.
16 Ratzinger, *Mary: The Church at the Source*, 15.

human role in the cosmic liturgy. As the *Catechism* observes, "Through his very bodily condition [man] sums up in himself the elements of the material world. Through him they . . . can raise their voice in praise *freely* given to the Creator."[17] "Nature prays with all of its existence," says the future John Paul II. "It is simply that the prayers of all non-human things are unexpressed! They're unformulated! The point is for human persons to formulate them."[18] This is what happens in the Eucharistic liturgy: through our freedom, in the offering of bread and wine "the whole of creation loved by God is presented to the Father . . . in thanksgiving for all that God has made good, beautiful, and just in creation and in humanity."[19] Here, at the climactic moment of the liturgy, a "morsel of bread is more real than the universe."[20]

But why bread and wine? What special qualities do they possess to become such a holy offering, to become *"the sacrament of the Bridegroom and of the Bride,"* to quote John Paul II's description of the Eucharist once again?[21] To provide at least some food for thought (pardon the pun) in answer to this question, we have to enter into creation's love song more deeply.

The Sacrificial Offering of Nature's Nuptials

"Hear this! A sower went out to sow. . . . And some seed fell on rich soil and produced fruit" (Mk 4:3, 8).

---

17 CCC 364, emphasis added.
18 Wojtyla, *God Is Beauty: A Retreat on the Gospel and Art*, 57–58.
19 CCC 1359.
20 John Paul II, *The Place Within*, 11.
21 John Paul II, *Mulieris Dignitatem* 26.

"The kingdom of heaven may be compared to someone who
sowed good seed in his field" (Mt 13:24).

"Of its own accord the land yields fruit, first the blade, then
the ear, then the full grain in the ear" (Mk 4:28)

"The kingdom of heaven is like a mustard seed" (Mt 13:31).

"There was a landowner who planted a vineyard" (Mt 21:33).

"The harvest is abundant, but the laborers are few" (Mt 9:37).

"Consider the fig tree and all the other trees" (Lk 21:29).

"Every tree is known by its own fruit" (Lk 6:44).

"Consider how the wild flowers grow" (Lk 12:27).

Why did Christ speak so frequently about nature's fertility?
Because natural fecundity is in some way the starting point
of all theophany. Christ speaks of natural fecundity again and
again so that we might glimpse the mystery of supernatural
fecundity; so that we might come to understand that "God
sent his only-begotten Son into the world so that we might
have *life* through him" (1 Jn 4:9). For "just as from the heavens
the rain and snow come down and do not return there till they
have watered the earth, making it fertile and fruitful, giving
seed to the one who sows and bread to the one who eats, so
shall my word be that goes forth from my mouth; it shall not
return to me empty, but shall do what pleases me, achieving
the end for which I sent it" (Is 55:10–11).

"He who sows good seed is the Son of Man . . . and the
good seed the children of the kingdom" (Mt 13:37–38).
We also read in Scripture that this *life* sown by the eternal
Bridegroom is "the light of men" (Jn 1:4), the light that

illuminates what it means to be human, why we are here, and what our destiny is. Those with eyes to see can recognize a reflection of this light in all of nature's fertility. As we learned in Chapter 5, the Old Testament begins with the theophany of nature's fertility culminating in the theophany of human fertility: "in the image of God he created them [as] male and female . . . and God said to them: Be fertile and multiply" (Gen 1:27–28). The New Testament, in turn, begins with human fertility culminating in Mary's fertility opened to the *infinitely fertile power* of God's eternal Fatherhood. In this way, as the *Catechism* keenly expresses it, carrying the eternal Son in her womb, Mary became "the burning bush of the definitive theophany."[22] In other words, as we learned previously, pregnant Mary became the definitive icon of what it means for the human person to "be filled with all the fullness of God" (Eph 3:19).

The whole of the above sequence (nature's fertility culminating in human fertility culminating in Mary's fertility opened to "the Lord, the giver of Life") is re-presented sacramentally in the liturgy. As Saint John Paul II proclaimed, "The same *logic of love* presides at the Incarnation of the Word in Mary's womb, and at his becoming present in the Eucharist."[23] And that *logic of love* is precisely what nature's fecundity whispers, which is why we place precisely *that* on the altar. In turn, "the birth of Jesus Christ," Saint Paul VI tells us, "will be renewed in a mystical and sacramental form, with a mysterious realism on this altar."[24] For that mystery of divine-human

---

22 CCC 724.
23 John Paul II, Holy Thursday homily, 2004.
24 Paul VI, homily at Midnight Mass of the Solemnity of the Nativity of the Lord, December 25, 1971,

fecundity to be renewed, however, we must offer the Father what he has first offered us: the fecundity of the earth, or, we might say, the fecundity of nature's nuptials . . .

> Blessed are you, Lord, God of all creation,
> for through your goodness we have received the bread we
>   offer you:
> fruit of the earth and work of human hands,
> it will become for us the bread of life.

> Blessed are you, Lord God of all creation,
> for through your goodness we have received the wine we
>   offer you:
> fruit of the vine and work of human hands,
> it will become our spiritual drink.[25]

Have you ever pondered the significance of the fact that at the high point of Christian worship, we place the *fruit* of nature's nuptials on an altar of *sacrifice*? "Fruit" comes from the Latin *fructus*, which means an enjoyment, delight, or satisfaction proceeding/harvested from the earth. "Sacrifice" comes from the Latin *sacra-facere* which means to make sacred, holy. In the Eucharistic liturgy, enjoyments proceeding from nature's nuptials become sacred in a manner *exceeding all human imagination.* Here, as the result of the divine power of the Eucharistic prayer flowing through the priest's spiritual fatherhood, nature's fertility not only "points" to the eternal life that is Christ (as in the Lord's parables), it undergoes an

---

25 Prayer of preparation of the altar and the offerings, *The Roman Missal*, trans. International Commission on English in the Liturgy, 3rd typical ed. (United States Conference of Catholic Bishops, 2011).

astounding transubstantiation (change in substance) and actually *becomes* that life.

But there's more—so much more—to this great mystery of nature's nuptials coming to ultimate fruition in the liturgy! Bread comes from the crushed and baked *seed* of the wheat stalk. In fact, the essential part of the seed for the purpose of making bread is called the *endosperm* ("the seed within the seed"). Wine comes from the crushed and fermented ovary of the grapevine. We don't tend to think of it very often, but that's what grapes *are*. Furthermore, both wheat stalks and grapevines are flowering plants—flowers, themselves, being one of nature's most readily displayed and radiantly beautiful reproductive organs. All these symbols of fertility play an integral role in the Eucharistic liturgy.

Have you ever noticed that the chalice is shaped like a flower? The very word "chalice" comes from the Latin *calyx*, which also refers to the cup of a flower.[26] The calyx of the flower supports and protects the flower's petals and ovary so that pollination and fertilization can take place. As morning yields its dew and the flower opens to the heat of the rising sun, the petals capture the dewdrops—moisture being essential for the life and fertility of the flower—and the flower's fragrance is "wafted abroad" (Song 4:16) in order to attract bees or other pollinators. In turn, when the priest calls upon the Holy Spirit (this symbolism is all the more clear when he's facing the rising sun), we witness the consummate moment of grace perfecting nature:

---

26 My deep gratitude goes to Father Boniface Hicks for the homily he delivered in which I first learned of the connection between the chalice and the calyx of a flower. That one homily opened up a new world for me.

Make holy, therefore, these gifts, we pray,
by sending down your Spirit upon them like the dewfall,
so that they may become for us
the Body and Blood of our Lord Jesus Christ.[27]

Dewfall has an ancient biblical history as a symbol of heavenly blessing and supernatural fecundity: "In holy splendor, . . . like the dew I have begotten you" (Ps 110:3); "Let justice descend, you heavens, like dew from above. . . . Let the earth open and salvation bud forth" (Is 45:8); "For there will be a sowing of peace: the vine will yield its fruit, the land will yield its crops, and the heavens will yield their dew" (Zech 8:12).[28] As we learned in Chapter 4, at the Annunciation, the earth that opens to the "dew from above" is Mary, and the salvation that buds forth is Jesus. After the same pattern, in the liturgy, with the earth having yielded its wheat and its grapes—and having become, with the work of human hands, bread and wine—the heavens then yield their dew, and nature's nuptials *become* the nuptials of heaven and earth. Here, when the Holy Spirit falls upon them "like the dewfall," the fruit of the earth and the fruit of the vine *actually become the fruit of Mary's womb!*

We can see that when Jesus invites us to consider how the wild flowers grow, he's not merely bidding us to become better botanists; he's luring us into loving the liturgy. He's inviting us into nature's love song. It's not merely for the sake of decoration, after all, that we place nature's most beautiful reproductive organs (flowers) around the altar at Mass. Nor

---

27 Eucharistic Prayer II, *The Roman Missal.*
28 For a few other examples, see Genesis 27:28, 33:13; Deuteronomy 32:2; Psalm 133:3; Hosea 14:5.

is it without great significance that the Church prescribes candles for liturgical use that are "the work of bees and of your servants' hands," as the Exsultet of the Easter Vigil proclaims. These are all potent and profound *symbols* (think once again of the broken ring revealing what cannot be seen) of what liturgy *is* as the consummation of the natural world's nuptials in the nuptials of divinity and humanity.

The Serpent and the Garden and the Seed

Some have wondered if all this glorified talk of nature's fertility doesn't border on the idolatry of the ancient fertility cults explicitly condemned in the Bible.[29] Keep in mind that, because the devil doesn't have his own clay, all he can do in promoting false worship is mock true worship. The offering of nature's fertility to God in Christian liturgy is, in fact, the *setting aright* of the serpent's mockery found in those ancient cults. Benedict XVI observes that the serpent itself "is a figure derived from oriental fertility cults that fascinated Israel and that were a constant temptation to forsake the mysterious covenant with God."[30] That mysterious covenant with God is *symbolized* in the fruitfulness of the created world. While the false worship induced by the serpent *idolizes* the fruit of the earth and the work of human hands, the true worship to which the Holy Spirit invites us *liturgizes* the fruit of the earth and the work of human hands. The former leads to the horrors of temple prostitution and child sacrifice, while the latter leads to the glories of the divine-human nuptials consummated in the sacrifice of the Mass.

---

29 See Leviticus 18:21, Deuteronomy 16:21 and 23:17, and 2 Kings 23:4–7 for some examples.

30 Benedict XVI, General Audience of February 6, 2013.

Alexander Schmemann observes that the "liturgy is, before everything else, the joyous gathering of those who are to meet the risen Lord and to enter with him into the bridal chamber."[31] And theologian Adam Cooper reminds us that in "both Israelite and Christian worship, there has always been a sense that what takes place in the words and rites of the liturgy is, as it were, an active 'letting be' for God to enter into an erotic, nuptial bond of union with his Bride, the new Jerusalem."[32] The wisdom of Sirach paints a marvelous picture for us of this active, bridal posture of "letting be." Here we see both how the flowers of the earth (nature's fertility) symbolize and participate in this cosmic liturgy and how we are called to draw out the song of praise at the base of all things:

Listen to me, my faithful children: open up your petals,
like roses planted near running waters;
Send up the sweet odor of incense,
break forth in blossoms like the lily.
Raise your voices in a chorus of praise;
bless the Lord for all his works!
Proclaim the greatness of his name, loudly sing his praises,
with music on the harp and all stringed instruments;
sing out with joy as you proclaim:
The works of God are all of them good;
he supplies for every need in its own time. (Sir 39:13–16)

John Paul II wrote in his poem *Shores of Silence* that "there is life in the open rose, as there is God descending from

---

31 Schmemann, *For the Life of the World*, 29.
32 Adam Cooper, *Holy Eros: A Liturgical Theology of the Body* (Angelico Press, 2014), 23.

the heights."[33] Mary is that open rose. She is the "Mystical Rose" who opened her petals before the heat of the rising sun, receiving heavenly dew descending from the heights.[34] She is the Bride who called upon the wind of the Spirit to "blow upon [her] garden" that "its fragrance might be wafted abroad" (Song 4:16). Indeed, what do visionaries and others who've experienced encounters with Mary smell in her presence? They report the mysterious scent of roses. In actuality, however, Mary doesn't smell like roses. Respecting the proper cosmological order reveals that *roses smell like Mary*. Mary is not imitating the lower forms of fecundity; their fragrant fecundity points to and culminates in hers!

When the Church prays the words of Psalm 67:6, "The earth has yielded its fruits" (typically prayed on Marian feast days), she knows that these words are fulfilled in the fruit of Mary's womb. Mother earth was made to bear the second Person of the Trinity in her depths. This is "the end for which 'in the beginning God created the heavens and the earth,'" as the *Catechism* affirms.[35] Hence, Mary is the pinnacle of the natural order. She "concentrates and condenses" in herself "all the wonders of the world."[36] All of nature's life-givingness is consummated and brought to ultimate fruition in her "garden," which, as the new Eden (the new "paradise of fertile delights"), brings forth the New Adam.

---

33 John Paul II, *The Place Within*, 8.

34 Adapting the passage we've already quoted from Isaiah, the Church prays in preparation for Christmas: "Drop down dew from above, you heavens, and let the clouds rain down the Just One; let the earth be opened and bring forth a Savior" (Entrance Antiphon, Fourth Sunday of Advent). Mary is that "opened earth"!

35 CCC 280.

36 Arminjon, *The Cantata of Love*, 296

"As Eden was the Paradise of Creation, Mary is the Paradise of the Incarnation, and in her as a Garden was celebrated the first nuptials of God and man."[37]

Mary is thus the Bride in whom these prophetic words find their fulfillment: "Your navel is a bowl well rounded with no lack of wine, your belly a heap of wheat surrounded by lilies" (Song 7:3). "Here the images seem to be daring," says Father Blaise Arminjon in his widely read commentary on the Song of Songs. "But there is no reason to be shocked. . . . The Word of God is not ashamed of what God has created." With these images, it seems the author of the Song "wishes to convey the fecundity of the Bride." Arminjon elaborates:

> The Holy Land is a country of wine and wheat, "a land of . . . bread and of vineyards" (2 Kings 18:32). Now the "wedded" land will know on that day of the messiah an extraordinary fecundity of wheat and wine. . . . And this will be attested to at the advent of the messiah by the two miracles of the wine streaming at the wedding feast of Cana and the multiplication of the loaves. . . . Wonderful fecundity of the Bride-earth-Israel, wonderful fecundity of the love union between the Bride and the Bridegroom also symbolized by these images . . . expressly associated with the navel and belly of the Bride. Cup "not lacking in wine" (at Cana wine was lacking, and Jesus gave a wine that will not lack) and "heap of wheat," these two expressions of superabundance indicate the inexhaustible nature of that fecundity. . . . And in this respect, it is infinitely suggestive for us that in this

37 Fulton Sheen, *Those Mysterious Priests* (Doubleday, 1974), 307.

passage of the Song this fecundity is associated with . . . the two eucharistic symbols.[38]

As we stated above, the Eucharistic liturgy represents the consummate moment of grace perfecting nature—which, in the literal sense of "nature," we shall recall, means the consummate moment of grace perfecting the manner in which we are born (*natus*). Just as the supernatural fecundity of the Bride/Church is signified in a woman's natural capacity to become a mother, the supernatural fecundity of the Bridegroom/Christ is signified in a man's natural capacity to become a father. According to the logic of the mega mystery of Ephesians 5:31–32 (the two becoming one flesh is a "mega mystery" referring to Christ and the Church), the contribution unique to a woman *and* the contribution unique to a man are required in both the natural and supernatural expressions of communion and fecundity. It's the Bridegroom "who sows good seed" (Mt 13:37) or inseminates; it's the Bride who receives the seed within and conceives new life. This is where the sexual difference fulfills its decisive purpose.

Wheat and wine represent the bridal fecundity of creation-earth-Church. When an ordained priest prays the words of consecration over them, a spiritual "power goes out" from his masculine body that sacramentally represents the fecundity of the heavenly Bridegroom poured into the womb of the Bride (see Lk 8:46). In short, the sacramental priesthood demands the ability to *sow the spiritual seed* that generates eternal life within the Bride's mystical garden/womb. This is why a

---

38 Arminjon, *The Cantata of Love*, 304, 306–7, 309.

man trains to be a priest in the *seminary* and, once ordained, is called *father*. It's true that in the corporate personality of the Church, every baptized person shares in the "priesthood of all believers," just as every baptized person shares in the "bridehood of all believers." But when a single member of the congregation is chosen to represent the Church as Bride, as in the role of a vowed nun, it must be a woman. Likewise, when a single member of the congregation is chosen to become a living sacrament of Christ as Bridegroom, as in the role of an ordained priest, it must be a man.[39]

Difference Is Very Good

Instead of despising and rebelling against the sexual difference as the modern world is hell-bent on doing, we would do far better to ask for the grace to recognize why God looked at this difference he had created and called it "very good" (Gen 1:31). When we fail to recognize the goodness of the sexual difference, we also fail to recognize the goodness of the difference it signifies: the difference between Creator and creature. Or, rather, failing to recognize the goodness of the sexual difference is evidence that we have *already* lost sight of the goodness of the difference between the Creator and the creature. Allow me to explain.

39 Limiting priestly ordination to men makes zero sense . . . *unless* . . . unless priesthood inherently expresses that which only men can do. Women can certainly do *most* of the things men can do, just as men can certainly do *most* of the things women can do. But men and women are not simply interchangeable. There is something only men can do (because they're men) and only women can do (because they're women) and they must do it together in order to be able to do it at all: only men can be fathers and only women can be mothers. We used to call this "the facts of life," but today, because we've embraced a new Gnosticism, the facts of life appear to be entirely up for grabs.

In the spousal imagery of the Scriptures, God is always the Bridegroom and humanity is always the Bride because the creature, by nature, is fundamentally *receptive* to the life-giving gift of the Creator. This fundamental difference represents, at God's loving initiative, a call to an eternally life-giving communion between Creator and creature, with God awaiting "the 'yes' of his creatures as a young bridegroom that of his bride."[40] Tempted, however, by the father of lies, we came to conceive of the Creator as a tyrant with a will to enslave us. Ever since, we've been seeking to eliminate the perceived threat, not by renouncing the deceiver's lie about God's character as tyrant, but by leveling the difference between Creator and creature in one of two ways: either by *raising ourselves up* to the level of God or by *pulling God down* to our level.

These attempts to level the difference between Creator and creature have, in turn, had a profound impact on the way human beings understand and live the sexual difference. Before I unfold that logic, however, I must acknowledge that the following observations concern fallen humanity in the collective sense. Hence, it would be inappropriate to infer specific knowledge of an individual's personal beliefs about the Creator-creature relationship based on the observations below. Nor can we impute culpability to individuals for whatever distorted sexual inclinations they might discover in themselves. Of course, we are responsible for whether we foster or resist such inclinations, and we must maintain with Saint John that these inclinations are "not from the Father." Rather, they come "from the world" (1 Jn 2:16)—the fallen

---

40 Benedict XVI, Lenten Message, 2007.

world that has resulted from humanity's collective distrust of the Creator. Whatever variety of distorted inclinations one may discover in his or her fallen humanity, we are all called with the help of God's grace to "channel [our] passions in a beautiful and healthy way, increasingly pointing them toward altruism and an integrated self-fulfillment."[41] Mindful of these important points, let's look now at the sexual logic of that collective distrust of the Creator.

In his letter to the Romans, Saint Paul rightly traces all the bad fruit of our distorted erotic passions to one source: the fact that we have "exchanged the truth about God for a lie" (Rom 1:25–28). Because the sexual relationship signifies the Creator-creature relationship, a culture will incarnate in the former the manner in which it skews the latter. For example, when we embrace the lie that God is a tyrant who wants to enslave the creature, that will be incarnated at the human level just as Genesis foretold: men will dominate and enslave women to gratify their lust (and women will manipulate men to satisfy their own lust in turn; see Gen 3:16).[42] When we reject our Bridal receptivity as creatures and raise ourselves to God's level as Bridegroom, that will be incarnated at the human level in the normalization of two bridegrooms (male homosexuality). Conversely, when we reject

---

41 Pope Francis, *Amoris Laetitia* 148.

42 In one concise sentence, Genesis states the tragic impact of the fall on the male-female relationship: "Your desire shall be for your husband and he will dominate you" (Gen 3:16). The Hebrew word translated as "desire" indicates a distorted, manipulative impulse on the woman's part, which corresponds (in its broken logic) to the fallen man's will to dominate and control woman. Here it is critical to remember Christ's all-important declaration: "in the beginning it was not so" (Mt 19:8), and the good news that he "came to restore creation to the purity of its origins" (CCC 2336).

God as Bridegroom and pull him down to our level as Bride, that will be incarnated at the human level in the normalization of two brides (female homosexuality).

These various incarnations of exchanging the truth about God for a lie have been wreaking havoc on God's original plan for our humanity ever since the Fall. But there is something unfolding today that has *never* happened in all of history: large, influential swaths of humanity have sought to eliminate the threat of a (falsely conceived) tyrannical God by eliminating the notion of God's existence altogether. As Cardinal Wojtyla observed, this is the ultimate goal of the anti-Word: to get man to deny the very existence of God. However, in earlier stages of history, an outright "denial of God is not possible because his existence is too apparent." At first, Lucifer could only go after God's character. "But the time has now come," observes Wojtyla: "this aspect of the devil's temptation has found the historical context that suits it." With the global spread of atheism, we "may now be wondering if this is the last lap along that way of denial which started out from around the tree of the knowledge of good and evil."[43]

And so we now have an unprecedented incarnation at the human level of this attempt to eliminate God altogether: the attempt to eliminate the sexual difference altogether. If there's no God, then there's certainly no "image of God" revealed in our creation as male and female that we must honor. Without God, we come to conceive of our humanity as a blank canvas upon which we, as lords of our own identity, can now paint ourselves however we see fit without any repercussions. This unprecedented global attack on the meaning of our sexual

---

43 Karol Wojtyla, *Sign of Contradiction* (Seabury Press, 1979), 30, 34, 35.

embodiment may well indicate that "we are experiencing the highest level of tension between the Word and the anti-Word in the whole of human history."[44]

The Good News revealed in the Word made flesh is this: there *is* a God, and he is *not* the tyrant we've conceived him to be. In fact, "God's very being is love. By sending his only Son and the Spirit of Love in the fullness of time, God has revealed his innermost secret: God himself is an eternal exchange of love, Father, Son and Holy Spirit, and he has destined us to share in that exchange."[45] God has entered the realm of the creature not to be served, but to serve; not to enslave, but to liberate; not to dominate but to invite us into his own eternal exchange of love. Hence, being in the bridal posture before him is *not* the threat we've conceived it to be either. The difference between the Creator and the creature is *very good*! It's precisely what affords the astounding *Communion* between God and man to which we are all invited.

Jesus Christ himself *is* that Communion; he is the God-Man. And Mary is *the Woman* who, representing the whole human race, trusted in God's "mad eros" for the creature, remained in the posture of Bride, and gave her complete "yes" to the divine marriage proposal. In Mary we see that we don't need to pull God down to our level: at her consent, God freely descended into her womb and made himself one of us. In Mary we see that we don't need to raise ourselves up to God's level: Mary's bodily Assumption into the Life of the Trinity reveals that God wants to raise us all up to participate in his own nature (see 2 Pt 1:4). In Mary, we see

44 Ibid., 34.
45 CCC 221.

that the difference between the Creator and the creature is a call to nuptial union, and it is *very good*. In turn, we see that the difference between male and female, as the primordial sacrament of the difference between Creator and creature, is also a call to nuptial union, and we long for that difference to be lived and celebrated as God always intended it to be.

Hence, the incarnation at the human level of embracing *the* Incarnation at the divine level is a readiness to submit all our sexual distortions and confusions—however they have manifested themselves in our own lives—to the powers flowing from Christ's bodily death and Resurrection in joyful hope of full restoration of God's original *very good* plan for creating us male and female. And this brings us back once again to the sound of music in the cosmic liturgy.

Silence, Shouting, and Song

We are created as male and female to participate freely in the divine love song latent in all of creation. Tuning in to that divine song, however, is impossible without the art of *listening* to the pregnant depths of the universe in contemplative silence. Tragically, in the modern world the ability to listen to those depths is being drowned out by the incessant noise pollution of false worship. These counterfeit liturgies, in turn, once they've misdirected eros and worked their degradations, generate that primal scream we discussed in the previous chapter.

It is into this mega misery that God descends in order to restore the mega mystery. Christ the Bridegroom's desire is made clear in the Song of Songs: "I have come to my garden, my sister, my bride. . . . Open to me!" (Song 5:1–2). When the Bride opens to the Bridegroom in the liturgy, humanity's primal scream is transformed back into the primordial song of the cosmic liturgy. Benedict XVI explains as follows:

> Mahatma Gandhi . . . refers to the three habitats of the cosmos and how each of these provides its own mode of being. The fish live in the sea and they are silent. The animals of the earth scream and shout; but the birds, whose habitat is in the heavens, sing. Silence is proper to the sea, shouting to the earth, and singing to the heavens. Human beings have a share in all three of them. They carry the depths of the sea, the burden of the earth, and the heights of the heavens in themselves, and for this reason, all three properties belong to them: silence, shouting, and singing. Today—I would like to add—we see that only the shouting is left for those humans without transcendence. . . . Right liturgy . . . restores totality to [those cut off from the Infinite]. It teaches them silence and singing again by opening to them the depths of the sea and teaching them to fly. . . . It brings the song buried in them to sound once more by lifting up their hearts [*sursum corda*]. . . . One recognizes right liturgy by the fact that it liberates us from ordinary, everyday activity and returns to us once more the depths and the heights, silence and song. One recognizes right liturgy in that it has a cosmic . . . character. It sings with the angels. It is silent with the expectant depths of the universe. And that is how it redeems the earth.[46]

And now our reflections in this chapter have come full circle. Liturgy redeems the earth by placing its fruits on an altar of sacrifice and inviting the divine *descent*: "Make holy these

---

46   Benedict XVI, *A New Song for the Lord*, 160.

gifts," the priest prays, "by sending down your Spirit upon them like the dewfall." The priest also prays in remembrance of "Christ's death and his descent to the realm of the dead." Then we celebrate the *ascent*, in which all of creation is lifted up with Christ into God's eternity, when the priest proclaims the Lord's "wondrous Resurrection and Ascension into heaven."[47]

Notice that descent always precedes ascent. If we are to experience the joy of ascending with Christ into his heavenly Life, we must first be willing to descend with him into his hellish death: we must accept the *asceticism* (discipline) of the Cross if we are to experience the *aestheticism* (beauty) of the Resurrection. This, in fact, is the litmus test for whether we are rejoicing rightly in the attraction of eros to beauty: true beauty, and true attraction to it, always involves the element of the Cross. We will explore what this means in more detail in our final chapter.

INTO THE MYSTIC

1. What's something you learned in this chapter that you hadn't known before?

2. Think of a time in your life when you were deeply moved by the gift of music. Have you ever considered that God was wooing you? Have you ever considered that musical instruments are a way of eliciting the sacred sounds that God has hidden within his creation?

3. Have you ever heard that prayer, properly understood, is nothing other than becoming a longing for God? How

---

47 Eucharistic Prayers II, III, IV, *The Roman Missal.*

might this impact the way you pray from now on? How can you facilitate getting in touch with your deepest desires and opening them to God as prayer?

4. What is your favorite place in God's creation? Do you especially love vacationing at a lake, at the beach, the bay, the mountains? Did you ever enjoy collecting little bits of God's creation like rocks or flowers or seashells? Did you have a favorite tree you liked to climb as a child? How might God have been wooing you into the mystery of the liturgy through your attraction to these things?

CHAPTER 8

Open Wide
Your Mouth and
I Will Fill It

Faith and chaste eros are the same thing . . .

—DR. TIMOTHY PATITSAS[1]

It may seem curious that in a book about the sacredness of eros we have not used the word "chaste" until now. The delay is due to how much baggage is typically attached to the word.

As we stated in Chapter 1, our pornographic culture has grievously bastardized the erotic, leaving our understanding of eros in critical need of rehabilitation. Similarly, both the large swath of Christians who have lived as functional Gnostics, as well as those people on the other extreme who promote the unleashing of an inverted eros as the key to human happiness, have grievously bastardized the word "chastity." As a result,

---

1   Patitsas, "Chastity and Empathy," 42, n23.

the virtue without which we cannot experience the joy, freedom, and fulfillment for which we long has taken on the bitter
taste of something repressive and dehumanizing. Having spent
seven chapters attempting to rebuild a proper understanding
of eros, we now have the necessary foundation to understand
what chastity truly is, and what it is not.

Eros in Its Holy Form

Chastity comes from the Latin *castus*, which means "pure."
Christian purity is not prudishness or puritanism. It does not
involve the rejection or repression of our passions, but rather
the redemption and transformation of them, redirecting eros
toward a proper delight in the true, the good, and the beautiful. "Purity is the glory of the human body before God,"
affirms John Paul II. "It is the glory of God in the human
body, through which masculinity and femininity are manifested."[2] Hence, the virtue of chastity or purity of heart is
what enables us to reclaim the human body and the entire
physical world as theophany: "Blessed are the pure in heart,
for they shall see God" (Mt 5:8).

"Chastity means the successful integration of sexuality
within the person and thus the inner unity of man in his
bodily and spiritual being."[3] In short, chastity is eros in its
holy form. And just as eros encompasses sexual desire but is
broader, chastity includes the proper use of our sexual powers, but is more expansive. In fact, if we limit chastity to
sexual purity, we'll fail at both.[4] The chaste person is the
one who has entrusted the hunger of his or her heart to the

2   John Paul II, TOB 57:3.
3   CCC 2337.
4   Patitsas, "Chastity and Empathy," 6.

One who alone can satisfy it, heeding the Lord's invitation: "Open wide your mouth and I will fill it" (Ps 81:11).

For chastity to flourish, our eyes must be opened to the fullest dimensions of theophany. We must become sensitive to the promptings of divine Beauty that never cease in us and all around us, because Beauty is the only thing that can keep the eye chaste.[5] As the English poet John Donne exclaimed, "Except you enthrall me, never shall be free/Nor ever chaste, except you ravish me!"[6] Chastity, in its more mature form, then, is not a closing of our eyes to earthly beauty, but an opening of our eyes to their widest capacity so that earthly beauty leads the heart to be ravished by heavenly Beauty.

Lust involves a loss of that vision, a closing of the eyes to the sacramental manner in which earthly beauty is meant to lead us to heavenly Beauty. Recall how the prophet Daniel describes the inner corruption of those elders who lusted after Joakim's wife Susanna: "They would not allow their eyes to look to heaven," he says (Dan 13:9). What an insightful understanding of lust! If those men had known chaste eros, Susanna's beauty would have led them on pilgrimage to the Beauty of heaven. But "they perverted their thinking" (Dan 13:9) and refused the invitation to theophany that God had written into her body.

For those bound in their hearts by lust, the Old Testament injunction "turn away your eyes from a shapely woman" (Sir 9:8) retains all its wisdom. However, Christ's words about the sinfulness of looking lustfully (see Mt 5:28) are not merely an admonition to "turn away." As John Paul II explains, Christ's words are "an invitation to a pure way of

---

5   See ibid., 7.

6   John Donne, "Batter My Heart, Three-Person'd God."

looking at others, capable of respecting the spousal meaning of the body."[7] For in Christ we encounter "the possibility and the necessity of transforming what has been weighed down by the [lust] of the flesh."[8] While the road to mature chastity typically begins with averting one's stunted gaze from "too much" beauty, it leads to becoming one "whose eye is true . . . who sees what the Almighty sees, enraptured and with eyes unveiled" (Num 24:3–4). "Learning the dignity of the human person at the school of beauty takes a long time; it requires patience and constancy," as Stanislaw Grygiel rightly observes. However, as he also maintains: "Lowering our eyes at the sight of a beautiful body breaks off the path to knowing the truth that begins to reveal itself in that body." Shunning the beauty of the body in this way is a form of what he calls "sarcophopia": fear of the body and the mega mystery it proclaims. Such fear "devastates our society today."[9]

Mature chastity is mature sensuality: it makes us sensitive to how authentic beauty "tastes" and "smells" and "feels." To the degree that we are familiar with its flavor, aroma, and texture, illusory beauty—which attempts to sweep us away with the allure of its many false promises—becomes bitter, rank, and abrasive. Putting a biblical image to it, chaste eros senses the keen distinction between the pure beauty of the Bride/Jerusalem who rouses and attracts us to eternal life, and the illusory beauty of the whore/Babylon who seduces the nations and brings the world to ruin (see Rev 18–19).[10]

7   John Paul II, *Veritatis Splendor* 15.

8   John Paul II, TOB 47:5.

9   Grygiel, *Discovering the Human Person in Conversation with John Paul II*, 46, 74, 10.

10   John Paul II pointed out the difference between the Bride and "the hostile

Dostoevsky was speaking of authentic Beauty, of course, when he said, famously, that in the end the world will be saved by Beauty. Conversely, it's our stubborn clinging to illusory beauty that condemns us by paralyzing our true humanity. The rest of this chapter will explore how to tell the difference.

A Beauty-First Approach to Chastity

Recall that we have three basic choices with our erotically charged embodiment as male and female: idolize, despise, or liturgize. It's our functional Gnosticism that considers chastity to be primarily a suspicion toward or even a "sarcophobic" *despising* of the sexual and the erotic. Nothing could be further from the truth. To the degree that we recognize and live the body as the soul of Christianity, we will discover that chastity is the *liturgizing* of eros. The goal of both chastity and liturgizing eros is to redirect our rocket engines toward the stars, toward that for which our humanity is destined: bodily participation as male and female in the eternal ecstasy of the Trinitarian exchange via the marriage between Christ, the Bridegroom, and the Church, his Bride. This is what makes faith and chaste eros *the same thing*. Both, in their deepest essence, are the openness of the human heart—in all its poverty, need, and longing—to the riches of the divine gift granted in the liturgy: eternal life.[11]

and furious presence" of Babylon as follows: the woman clothed with the sun "is endowed with an inner fruitfulness by which she constantly brings forth children of God." In contrast, Babylon embodies "death and inner barrenness." General Audience address, February 7, 2001.

11 John Paul II wrote that "*faith*, in its deepest essence, is *the openness* of the human heart to the gift: *to God's self-communication in the Holy Spirit*," *Dominum et Vivificantem* 51.

And this makes chastity, as the *Catechism* affirms, "a promise of immortality."[12] In other words, it is a promise that the
cry of eros will not go unsatisfied. Far from extinguishing
the erotic cry of the heart, authentic chastity aims at *infinitiz-
ing* it. Here, renouncing all attachments to *false infinities*, we
learn to orient eros toward the *real thing*, transforming eros
itself into an all-consuming passion for God. This "demands
an intense spiritual commitment, and is no stranger to painful purifications," as Saint John Paul II explains. But these
purifications eventually render us "wholly possessed by the
divine Beloved, vibrating at the Spirit's touch" and overwhelmed by "the ineffable joy experienced by the mystics as
'nuptial union.' How can we forget here," the Polish pope
asks, "among the many shining examples, the teachings of
Saint John of the Cross and Saint Teresa of Avila?"[13]

Sadly, many have forgotten the truth to which these saints
(and so many others) attest. Patitsas summarizes their collective wisdom well: "The only cure for bad eros is good eros,
and plenty of it."[14] We cure *bad* eros not with the *sad* eros of
a Gnostic negation; we cure *bad* eros with the *mad* eros of a
soaring sublimation—raising it up, making it sublime. We
must allow God's grace to enflame holy eros within us by
entering ever more deeply into the *sursum corda* ("lift up your
hearts") of the liturgy.[15] This can be a very painful process,

---

12 CCC 2347.

13 John Paul II, *Novo Millennio Ineunte* 33.

14 Patitsas, "Chastity and Empathy," 60.

15 Commenting on the sad state of affairs in the Church today, a priest
friend of mine once lamented that if he were to put a "truth-o-meter"
on people's hearts during the *sursum corda* ("Lift up your hearts," says
the priest, and the people respond, "We lift them up to the Lord"), he
thought the needle on the meter would barely register a signal.

and the father of lies is ever-ready to tempt us into believing it is an impossible one. But far more painful, far more debilitating, is the lot of those who fall into this temptation and remain enslaved by disordered eros. It is truly possible and liberating to the core to make our bodies instruments of liturgy—that is, to learn the way of loving the Lord with all our heart, all our soul, all our mind, and all our strength. In doing so, says Patitsas, "we arrive at total eros for God. This all-consuming eros for Christ and the Holy Trinity is, as we have said, chastity."[16]

The critical point here is that we overcome evil with good, as Saint Paul says (see Rom 12:21). This is why a *sin-first* approach to chastity never works: "don't" becomes our only offering. When our focus is on what to avoid rather than on what to embrace, Christianity eventually collapses into a rigid and vapid moral system making the battle for chastity *de*structive rather than *con*structive. Negating eros only stokes the fires of its evil twin (lust). Instead, we must affirm eros in its holy form, stoking the fires enflamed by theophany; we must replace a *sin-first* approach to chastity with a *beauty-first* approach. This means, once again, we have to recover a sacramental vision of the world so our eyes are opened to how beauty leads to Beauty, eros leads to Eros. This doesn't happen without real interior struggle and intense spiritual battle, of course, but here our effort becomes not a striving to meet a moral imperative. Rather, it becomes a reorientation of desire toward the "mega mystery" that is infinitely *more Beautiful*, infinitely *more Attractive* than anything other for which eros might mistakenly think it yearns.

16 Patitsas, "Chastity and Empathy," 45.

In the end, these are our only two choices when it comes to chastening eros: moralism or mysticism. Christianity is an invitation to the latter, *not* the former. Indeed, the *Catechism* affirms that baptism, for everyone, is a call to the mystical life. This doesn't mean we should all expect to experience the bleeding wounds of Christ or bodily levitations. These extraordinary signs of the mystical life "are granted only to some for the sake of manifesting the gratuitous gift given to all."[17] And the gratuitous gift given to all is precisely the privilege of carrying in our bodies the death of the Lord so that his resurrected life might also be manifested in our bodies (see 2 Cor 4:10). As bad eros is crucified in us (see Gal 5:24), good eros is also resurrected in us, and to the degree that good eros flourishes in our hearts, bad eros loses its allure. Like a compass, even if spun, our hearts return to True North.[18]

Aligning Eros with Logos

In short, we experience chastity in as much as we align eros with *Logos*, opening our yearning to the infinite love flowing from the body of Christ. Here we must recognize that chastity is not something we first *do*. It is something we first *let be done unto us*. From all eternity, Christ himself is in this primarily receptive posture before the love of the Father, and that is what enables him, in turn, to pour that very love on us: "As the Father has loved me, so I have loved you" (Jn 15:9). In this same verse, Jesus then invites us to *remain* or *abide* in this love. Only then does he say, "love one another as I have loved you" (Jn 15:12).

17 CCC 2014.
18 See Patitsas, "Chastity and Empathy," 5, 40, 51–52, 58.

We see a basic principle at work here: we cannot give what we do not have; we cannot love as Christ loves (with a *mad eros*) if his love is not abiding in us. The Word becomes flesh so that divine love can be poured into us bodily. This is consummated in the Eucharistic liturgy. But then we are invited to allow that movement (Word made flesh) to be reversed in us, so that our flesh—without ceasing to be flesh—might become the divine Word; so that your flesh and mine might be taken up to participate with Christ in living and loving as he does. *This* is chastity. And Jesus invites us to this, he says, so that his joy may be in us and our joy may be complete (see Jn 15:10–12).

There's that little word "in" again that, as we said in Chapter 4, has the ability to open up an abyss of awe and wonder at the enormity of the privilege and promise offered us in the Gospel. Christ's joy *in* us: we are talking here about the ecstasy of knowing the infinite river of life and love flowing from the Father—*that's* Christ's joy. And it's offered to us! "The personal relation of the Son to the Father is something that man cannot conceive of nor the angelic powers even dimly see: and yet, the Spirit of the Son grants a participation in that very relation to us who believe that Jesus is the Christ and that we are born of God."[19]

To set our sights on so glorious a destiny, says Benedict XVI, is to stretch our lives out "towards the totality of all that is real, towards a boundless future," toward "a love without reserve—a love that is an immense affirmation of my existence and that discloses the fullness of all being to me in its breadth and depth." In and through this blissful affirmation "the Creator

19 CCC 2780.

of all things says to me, 'All that is mine is yours' (Lk 15:31)." In turn, this infinite river of love "opens up to me the whole of everything, which through love becomes 'paradise.'"[20] This glorious paradise is chastity's destiny. And it is precisely our hopeful yearning for so glorious a destiny that makes us chaste (see 1 Jn 3:3). Furthermore, from within the piercing of this holy longing, we realize not only that we yearn for paradise, but that paradise yearns for us! Personifying paradise with vivid bridal imagery, Saint Ephrem proclaims, "Yes, Paradise yearns for the man whose goodness makes him beautiful; it engulfs him at its gateway, it embraces him in its bosom, it caresses him in its very womb; for it splits open and receives him into its inmost parts. Blessed is he who was pierced and so removed the sword from the entry to Paradise."[21]

As we glimpse the nuptial joy that awaits us in paradise, to the degree that we glimpse it, we also come to embrace "the way" to that joy: we must die with Christ if we are to live with him. "For the sake of the joy that lay before him he endured the cross" (Heb 12:2). "Whoever omits the cross omits the essence of Christianity (see 1 Cor 2:2)."[22]

The Way of Beauty Is the Way of the Cross

Christ crucified and risen is our measure and criterion for determining whether we are rejoicing rightly or wrongly in beauty—whether eros has gone *mad* or eros has gone *bad*. It's gone *mad* when it compels us to sacrifice ourselves for the true,

20 Benedict XVI, *The Yes of Jesus Christ*, 69.
21 Saint Ephrem the Syrian, *Hymns on Paradise* 2:1 as cited in *Magnificat*, June 2022, 143.
22 Joseph Ratzinger, "Address to Catechists and Religion Teachers," December 12, 2000.

the good, and the beautiful. It's gone *bad* when it compels us to sacrifice the true, the good, and the beautiful for ourselves.

As we observed when reflecting on my backyard redbud trees, dying and rising are written into the order of creation itself. That means the way of beauty is fraught with sufferings. The Beauty I long for lies *beyond* the beauty of those redbud trees, and the only portal into that great *beyond* is death and resurrection. To recognize this logic in all of creation—"unless a grain of wheat falls to the ground and dies, it remains just a grain of wheat" (Jn 12:24)—is to recognize the watermark of the *Logos* in all of creation. Hence, following this logic and embracing where it leads becomes synonymous with following Christ. Conversely, following Christ becomes synonymous with a journey of continual dying and rising.

The Gospel invites us along the way of learning how to rejoice freely and fully in the pleasures of finite beauty, but without clinging to them. Refusing to cling to finite beauty when it awakens our yearning for the Infinite involves a real internal "letting go"—a real death. But it's a death that trusts fully in resurrection. It's a letting go that liturgizes the longing, trusting that its fulfillment will be granted superabundantly in the eternal gift. In this way, all created beauty is set ablaze with the divine promise. As Olivier Clement observes, "Resurrection begins every time that a person plunges [beyond] this world's opaque, divisive, death-riddled modality into its Christ-centered modality." In this pass over, Clement continues, we encounter what Saint Maximus the Confessor described as "that 'ineffable and marvelous fire hidden in the essence of things, as in the Burning Bush.'"[23]

---

23 Clement, *The Roots of Christian Mysticism*, 268.

All of this means that *aestheticism* must be wed to a proper *asceticism*. In other words, our appreciation of beauty must be wed to a discipline that trains us in appreciating it openhandedly, holding it loosely. Jesus says to Mary Magdalene, "Do not cling to me, for I have not yet ascended to my Father" (Jn 20:17). Ultimately, the Lord desires us to cling to him "as closely as the loincloth clings to a man's loins" (Jer 13:11), as we discussed previously. The "not yet" in Christ's words to Mary Magdalene, however, indicate that this life is not the ultimate; we've not reached our destiny until we have ascended with Christ to the Father.[24] We get little tastes of our destiny in the finite beauty all around us, and we can and should savor these tastes inasmuch as they awaken the hope of experiencing Infinite Beauty (more accurately, we should savor the hope that these tastes awaken). But if we try to suck infinite satisfaction out of these little tastes, we will not only be sorely disappointed; we will also leave a wake of destruction in our paths.

The purpose of asceticism "is not to make persons and things [we find attractive] disappear from view; rather it purifies the relationship of the heart with all that exists, so that the heart may be where its treasure—the Lord—is."[25] Far from making us unfeeling, proper asceticism, observes Clement, makes us "infinitely vulnerable to the beauty of the world."[26] A properly disciplined eros, a chaste eros, is one set on pilgrimage. It freely, readily, and joyfully allows itself to be awakened by the delight of finite beauty, but without latching on. Chaste eros is always traveling upstream toward

24 When Philip says, "Lord, show us the Father and that will be enough for us" (Jn 14:8), that word "enough" can be understood as the fulfillment of all yearning.
25 Corbon, *The Wellspring of Worship*, 210.
26 Clement, *The Roots of Christian Mysticism*, 131.

beauty's Source, allowing the stream of created beauty to flow by without demanding more from it than it can provide.

That stream of created beauty is certainly good in itself, but because we're made for the Infinite, that which passes away cannot provide the satisfaction for which we yearn. Rather, it's granted by God as a preview of coming attractions and as an encouragement to *keep going*. In one of her official prayers after Communion, the Church proclaims to the Lord that "as we walk amid passing things, you teach us by them to love the things of heaven and hold fast to what endures." In a similar Prayer after Communion, the Church entreats: "May your people, O Lord, . . . with the needed solace of things that pass away . . . strive with ever deepened trust for things eternal." Notice that fleeting beauty provides a *needed solace* on our journey. But fleeting beauty never says, "You've arrived; *this* is what you're looking for." That's the voice of the deceiver.

Undisciplined eros isn't interested in a life of pilgrimage. It wants its satisfaction now. And so *aestheticism* without *asceticism* turns us into grubbers and thieves: when we find ourselves aroused by the attraction of the beautiful, we *take* it on our own terms and run off with it in order to consume it. It's the original sin: the tree was "pleasing to the eyes" and "desirable," so they "*took* some of its fruit, and ate it" (Gen 3:6). It's not that God doesn't want us to have what is pleasing and desirable. Rather, he is inviting us into a relationship of trust; he wants us to receive the object of our desire from his hand as a gift, because he knows full well that what we desire (infinite joy) only he can grant.

And here we find ourselves facing once again the basic problem of human existence: the heart demands infinity but cannot grant it; eros desires an eternal fulfillment of love and beauty—to "eat the sunrise"—but the very thing we need the most we cannot procure for ourselves; we have to wait for it to be *given*. And it is this fundamental dependence that generates a deep anger and rebellion. We might pretend that eros *is* content with those pleasures we can procure for ourselves, and we might spend our lives procuring them without requiring any pilgrimage of the heart into the mega mystery. But that leads to mega misery, as we've already seen. Conversely, we can peacefully accept our fundamental posture of dependence in faith, with open trust that the Power to which we're subject truly loves us and wants to grant us the infinite fulfillment we desire: "I treasure your promises in my heart, lest I sin against you" (Ps 119:11).

Here we see the choice that will determine our fundamental disposition toward existence: to accept either the paradigm of love and openness to the gift, or the paradigm of control and domination. In other words, to accept the paradigm of worshiping the Father in Spirit and in Truth (liturgy-Eucharist-thanksgiving), or the paradigm of being my own god and worshiping myself. At this point the relevance of "the way of the Cross" becomes clear. As Saint Paul tells us, Christ, who was himself God, did not consider equality with God something to be *grasped at*. Rather, he humbled himself, accepting the human condition of suffering and death, even the most gruesome experience of death: death on a cross (see Phil 2:6–8).

The struggle with suffering and death is the place of our real reckoning with existence. Here, despite all our denials, we are forced to face the fact that we are not in control, that life is not at our disposal. It is here, in the midst of our kicking and screaming, that Christianity reveals itself as "good news." Christianity proclaims that suffering and death have been conquered by Love's willingness to absorb them into itself in order to overcome them with something far more powerful: the infinity of Love. Suffering and death are not thereby erased, but, rather, they are transformed from within *by* Love *into* Love, thus losing their "sting" (see 1 Cor 15:55).

The Christian is the one who knows that he can unite the constantly experienced truth that "I am not Lord of my life" with the truth that "a Love that is stronger than death *is* Lord of my life." Man can be at peace with his own existence only inasmuch as he trusts in this "unexacted gift of love," says Ratzinger. He continues: "Man's enemy, death, that would waylay him to steal his life, is conquered at the point where one meets the thievery of death with the attitude of trusting love, and so transforms the theft into increase of life. The sting of death is extinguished in Christ, in whom the victory was gained through the plenary power of love unlimited. Death is vanquished where people die with Christ and into him."[27]

Chastity's Trial Is the Cross

It is an illusion to think we can have beauty on non-crucified terms. To wrench beauty away from the *Logos*—away from the logic of the Cross—is to cut beauty off from its Source, which is why stolen beauty withers very quickly into something ugly. And so we must come to terms, again and again, with the fact that loving something beautiful always involves the Cross, because the *Logos* is present behind and within everything. In fact, whether we know it or not, it is the *Logos*

---

27 Joseph Ratzinger, *Eschatology*, 97. Content in the preceding few paragraphs was adapted from pp. 96 and 97 of this book.

within that thing of beauty to which we are actually attract-ed. Our assent to that presence assures us that eros is aimed at its proper end: the Infinite "Other," the Beauty beyond.

Of course, for a culture immersed in the opaque worldview of the Enlightenment, there is no "beyond." Inasmuch as it wishes to stay closed in and closed off, such a culture is wary of too much beauty, for it threatens to open us up to a Reality beyond our control. And when beauty doesn't submit to our control, it renders us vulnerable to an eros we cannot satisfy on our own. Falling in love with beauty as theophany is the proof that we are breaking out of the prison of the Enlightenment and are ready and willing to be overwhelmed by an all-con-suming eros for the *Logos* behind and within everything.[28] But, once again, the only way of entrance into participation in the Beauty that *is* the *Logos* is death and resurrection.

Whenever the fulfillment of our heart's desires is held out to us apart from the logic of the Cross, we know *exactly* whose voice is behind that seduction: "Get behind me, Satan!" (Mt 16:23), exclaimed Jesus to Peter when the first of the apostles attempted to steer him around the Cross. Recognizing our poverty and our instinct toward self-preservation, we must ask for the grace not to be shaken by "the way" that leads to Life (see Mt 7:14). Only grace can enable us to endure the vi-sion of Christ crucified, and even more, to be willing to die along with him. Here, as Peter also learned, self-reliance and bravado—"Even if I have to die with you, I will not deny you" (Mt 26:35)—get us nowhere.

Timothy Patitsas wonders if our first parents may have fallen because they could not endure the vision of Christ

---

28 See Patitsas, "Chastity and Empathy," 49.

crucified.[29] To gain access to this intriguing line of thinking, we have to exchange a chronological way of perceiving salvation history for the scriptural view that presents Christ as "the firstborn of all creation" (Col 1:15) and as "the Lamb slain before the foundation of the world" (Rev 13:8). This evocative proclamation from the final book of the Bible indicates not only God's foreknowledge that the nuptials of divinity and humanity would be consummated through the Cross. It indicates a different reckoning of history that holds the crucified and risen Christ to be its Alpha and Omega (see Rev 22:13). Patitsas wonders if our first parents, in some mysterious way, might have been given a vision of this slain Lamb as the ultimate revelation of divine love. Is the horror of the Cross what shook their faith? Was fear of that horror what caused Adam to fall silent in the face of the diabolical attack against his bride? Is this what caused them to turn their eros away from the divine—the fact that they could not endure the stark and brutal reality that eros is consummated through the marriage bed of the Cross? Was it their rejection of Christ's nakedness that caused them to realize *they* were naked? Was it Christ's vulnerable exposure that caused them to hide? Was their *bad* eros the result of being scandalized by Christ's *mad* eros? Indeed, can anyone witness the mad eros of the Cross without being tempted toward an alternative means of fulfilling the heart's yearning?

The crucifixion of Christ, as Patitsas presents it, was the enemy's attempt to lure the Bride's eros away from her Bridegroom (here we should understand "Bride" in the collective sense of

29　See ibid., 16, 20, 21 for his reflections from which I draw in the next few paragraphs.

all humanity). As such, the unleashing of hell on the Bridegroom in his crucifixion could be understood as an attempt to thwart the Bride's chastity. Chastity, as the purified form of eros, is the unswerving love-filled gaze of the Bride upon her Bridegroom, a gaze that follows the Lamb *wherever* he goes (see Rev 14:4). If prayer is eros for God, then chaste eros means to "pray without ceasing" (1 Thes 5:17). It means to keep eros aimed at the mega mystery of Christ and the Church, knowing full well that that marriage is consummated on a bed of agony. The moment the Cross enters the picture, we are sorely tempted to take eros in another direction. We are drawn to Beauty, but as soon as the Cross-within-Beauty comes into focus, we falter in our vision and are tempted to avert our faces in hopes that we can attain Beauty without suffering.

At the foot of the Cross, ever open to divine grace, "the Woman" (representing the Church and all humanity as the Bride) is the one who bears this temptation without averting her gaze. In union with the New Adam, who does not rebel at the prospect of his crucifixion, the New Eve endures the horror of beholding the slain Bridegroom with her eros fixed on Beauty in its most distressing disguise: "There was nothing in his appearance to draw us to him" (Is 53:2). In this way, the gift of the New Adam, faithful in his love "to the end" (Jn 13:1), found a response in the New Eve, that was also faithful to the end. In turn, the New Adam's and the New Eve's fidelity to the full demands of chaste-eros becomes the counterpoint to the first man and woman's infidelity to those demands.[30]

---

30 While always maintaining that Christ is the *Savior* and Mary is the *saved*, we can recognize that as Christ is the counterpoint to Adam's sin, Mary is the counterpoint to Eve's. The Second Vatican Council reminds us of

So we can see that chastity is eros embracing the agonizing nuptials of the Cross as the way to the ecstatic nuptials for which we yearn. It is a heart that *abides* in Christ's eros, and in turn, *loves as he loves* (see Jn 15:9, 12). This, in fact, is the litmus test of chaste eros: its willingness to "abide" in the sufferings of love—not in some masochistic way, but in view of and with certainty of faith that the Cross is the only way to the joy of the resurrection: "I have told you this so that my joy may be in you and your joy may be complete" (Jn 15:11). Unchastity is the attempt to run off with the joys of eros while shirking its sufferings (if only we could see that to do so leads, in fact, to abject misery!). The Word was made flesh, and that Word is love *to the end*. The call to love in this way—the call to love chastely—is the call to allow our flesh to be transformed into that Word, and that involves a long journey of renouncing our attachments to every illusory anti-Word.

A Fasting That Is Also Feasting

The illusory anti-Word inserts itself into the created order by tempting us to absolutize the pleasures of this world, turning icons into idols. In turn, the cure for such idolatry is not to turn eros down, but to turn it up—way up! Only to the degree that eros is infinitized will we be liberated from the illusion that finite pleasures can satisfy us. A *beauty-first* rather than a *sin-first* approach to chastity means that we start by cultivating and not suppressing the divine gift of eros at work within us, so that we might reach an all-consuming eros for the Creator. To do so, however, we must be weaned from an all-consuming

Saint Irenaeus's declaration: "The knot of Eve's disobedience was untied by Mary's obedience; what the virgin Eve bound through her unbelief, the Virgin Mary loosened by her faith" (*Lumen Gentium* 56).

eros for creatures, and that means fasting and self-denial must be part of cultivating chaste eros. Because our fallen nature is bent on aiming our desire for the Infinite at the finite, the reorientation of eros cannot happen without tempering our participation in those creature comforts to which we can all too readily become attached. But how does saying no to food or other pleasures actually increase our eros for God?

First of all, we must firmly establish this fact in our minds: the authentic Christian practice of fasting is *not* rooted in suspicion toward or rejection of the physical world, the human body, or the pleasures of food and drink. No one enjoyed good food and good wine as much as Jesus did. How do we know? Because the Pharisees accused him of being a glutton and a drunkard (see Lk 7:34). They couldn't image *that much* enjoyment being anything else. But for Christ it was a holy feasting born from a holy fasting. That's the spirit in which we are called to fast. As the *Catechism* says, we fast to "prepare us for the liturgical feasts."[31] The liturgical calendar establishes a rhythm of fasting and feasting in our lives, with an emphasis on feasting. For example, *forty* days of fasting during Lent prepare us for *fifty* days of feasting during the Easter season. Without regular times of fasting, we eventually lose the joy of feasting. If we always feast, in a sense, we never feast. Only those who know how to fast properly know how to feast properly. Entering the rhythm of both is essential.

Furthermore, because the body is the sacrament of the spirit, fasting, if we allow it, can make us palpably aware not only of our physical hunger, but also of our deeper spiritual hunger—our hunger for God (eros). Conversely, when we always

31 CCC 2043.

satisfy our hunger—be it for food or any other finite delight—
it can drown out the cry of our hearts for infinite delight. "I
will certainly impose privation," says Saint Augustine, "but it
is so that . . . I may enjoy his delightfulness."[32] Here Augustine
is repeating the teaching of his mentor, Saint Ambrose, who
observes that "the mystic feast is prepared for by fasting. . . .
It is bought at the price of hunger, and the cup of sober intoxication is gained by thirst for heavenly sacraments."[33]

We become ensnared by the pleasures of this world whenever we treat them as a God-substitutes. Fasting from food
and abstaining from other pleasures "help us acquire mastery
over our instincts and freedom of heart."[34] It is precisely this
freedom of heart that enables us to "tear through the thicket
of signs to the Word's very center,"[35] liberating eros from
its attachment to finite beauty so it can be directed toward
Infinite Beauty. Detachment from created things does *not*
mean we become cold or unfeeling toward the beauty of this
world. Rather, as our tendency to absolutize the things of
this world is purged, we rediscover the very things we once
idolized as so many icons of the divine mystery. "Creation,
and other people in particular," John Paul II affirms, "not
only regain their true light, given to them by God the Creator, but, so to speak, they lead us to God himself."[36]

Chaste eros, then, is a cultivated ability to rise above the
clamoring of the world, to see through the illusory beauty

---

32 Saint Augustine, *Sermo* 400, 3, 3: PL 40, 708.
33 Saint Ambrose, *On Elijah and Fasting*, 10, 33, as cited in Clement, *The
    Roots of Christian Mysticism*, 124.
34 CCC 2043.
35 John Paul II, *The Place Within*, 55.
36 John Paul II, *Memory and Identity* (Rizzoli, 2005), 39.

it exalts and with which it seduces, so as to free oneself to look for and feast upon true beauty, which is *always* beauty-as-theophany. As I once heard it said, no one is so free as the person who desires what he truly desires. Perhaps that third helping of deliciousness is *not* what we really want. Perhaps the sadness we feel when a meal is *over* is an indication that we are created for something more than fleeting feasts; we are created to feast upon the eternal One who yearns to be feasted upon. Fasting trains us to recognize that we do not live by bread alone, but by every word that comes from the mouth of God (see Mt 4:4). And here's the mystery: every word that comes from *God's* mouth is summed up in the One Word—the One *Logos*—who humbles himself at every Mass to appear as bread we take into *our* mouths. Here, mouth to mouth with God, we experience true adoration (recall that *ad-ora* means "at the mouth") and divinization by digestion. This is the liturgical feast for which fasting prepares us.

We must remind ourselves, again and again, that fasting is all about feasting on divine Beauty, which nourishes us in love and humility. When we forget this, fasting quickly devolves into feasting on our own good impression of ourselves; our self-denials become mere spiritual calisthenics we endure to shore up a sense of our own spiritual "progress" and bolster our own ego. When such is the case, says Olivier Clement, fasting becomes "the most dangerous of idols." He then quotes an anonymous Desert Father, who warns of the "evil smelling breath" that such fasting produces, because, for all our self-imposed discipline, we "still lack what God is looking for—love and humility."[37] Ironically,

37 Clement, *The Roots of Christian Mysticism*, 153.

sin can lead to the virtue of humility, while virtue can breed the sin of pride. "Imagine two chariots," says Saint John Chrysostom. "Harness virtue and pride to one, sin and humility to the other. You will see the chariot drawn by sin [and humility] outstrip that of virtue [and pride]."[38] To fulfill the purpose of fasting is to feast on Christ so completely that we go *out from self*—out from pride and our own sense of moral "accomplishment"—in the ecstasy of knowing pure Beauty (recall that "ecstasy" is from the Greek *ekstasis*: "to go outside oneself").

We might say, as Patitsas suggests, that to fast is to be so overcome by eros for Christ that we forget to eat. To fast is to leave behind every partial beauty, every sacrament of Beauty, and leap into the abyss of Infinite Beauty itself.[39] This leap *is* the leap of faith. We cannot see Infinite Beauty with our eyes. But we *can* see signs of Infinite Beauty all around us, all the time. Can we trust in what those signs promise? Can we allow those signs to *split open* and pour out their divine contents upon us and within us? Can we let go of our need to be in control of our own satisfaction and open wide our mouths before the Lord so that he might fill them? If we entrust ourselves to the liturgical rhythm of fasting and feasting and let that rhythm have its way with us, it will take us on a journey "from the visible to the invisible, from the sign to the thing signified, from the 'sacraments' to the 'mysteries.'"[40]

Fasting is a death. Feasting is a rising. While they seem separate to us in our fallen state, they form a single twofold

---

38 Saint John Chrysostom, *On the Incomprehensibility of God*, 5, as cited in ibid., 154.
39 See Patitsas, "Chastity and Empathy," 55.
40 CCC 1075.

response to the beautiful. We know a thing to be truly beautiful because in the ecstasy of loving and desiring it we encounter the logic of the Cross and are invited to a self-denial that, properly cultivated, trains us to rejoice in that beauty without grasping at it possessively. To the extent that we've been trained by the promise of theophany, the tendency to grasp possessively at beauty fades happily away. Fasting becomes, simultaneously, the occasion to feast on the beauty of the sunrise and the promise it contains: "You will not be unhappy; the desire of your heart will be fulfilled, what is more, it is already being fulfilled."[41]

The tree said:
don't be afraid when I die—don't be afraid to die with me,
don't be afraid of death—look, I revive:
death only grazed my bark.
Don't be afraid to die with me and revive.[42]

41 John Paul II, Letter addressing the *Communion and Liberation* gathering in Rimini, Italy, August 2002.
42 John Paul II, *The Place Within*, 128.

INTO THE MYSTIC

1. What's something you learned in this chapter that you hadn't known before?

2. In what ways is the word "chastity" in need of rehabilitation in your own life? In what ways is your understanding of chastity "sin-first" rather than "beauty-first"? Have you ever understood faith and chaste eros to be the same thing, an openness of your whole being to the divine gift? Have you understood a chaste person to be one "whose eye is true . . . who sees what the Almighty sees, enraptured and with eyes unveiled" (Num 24:3–4)?

3. In what ways do you accept the paradigm of love and trusting in the gift, and in what ways do you tend toward the other paradigm of grasping, control, and domination? How are these different dispositions related to chastity and/or the lack thereof?

4. In what ways have you sought the pleasure and satisfaction of beauty in your life while denying the Cross within that beauty? How can fasting lead you to a proper feasting on beauty? Do you believe that God wants to satisfy your heart's yearning to participate in Beauty?

Allowing Ourselves to be Wooed

I conclude this book with a meditation on desire and beauty that I've summarized from a retreat given by my professor and mentor, with whom you have become familiar throughout this book, the late Monsignor Albacete. The wit, the style, the humor, and the insights below are all his. I've simply condensed and adapted them for the purpose of drawing this book to a close.[1] Indeed, what follows summarizes wonderfully what I've wanted to share with you.

One note is necessary to avoid confusion. The word "seduce" often has a negative connotation, implying that one is being lured into sin. Albacete obviously uses the word quite differently. Sinful seduction is the diabolic mockery of how the Lord woos our hearts through a powerful attraction to the beautiful. The prophet Jeremiah exclaims, "You seduced me, Lord, and I let myself be seduced" (Jer 20:7). May we not be afraid to allow ourselves to be seduced in the same way!

---

1   See Lorenzo Albacete, *Priesthood and the Human Vocation* (a retreat transcribed and published by the Communion and Liberation movement, 2009), 6, 7, 8, 12–13, 61, 70, 71, 72, 77, 80.

What defines our life is interest and attraction. What are we interested in or attracted to? If you are interested in absolutely nothing, you are not alive. Interest is a "looking for" . . . an impulse of your very existence, not just your mind; it's your whole self that somehow needs to know more, needs to see more, is in search of something more—the Mystery, the Unknowable . . . God. What does it mean to be "interested" in God? It's not just a theological interest, although that may be part of it. The fact that we intellectualize everything is a problem. What I'm talking about is a search upon which you embark because your very life is involved—pardon me for a vulgar term, but your "ass" is involved. If I do not embark on this search, I've been dulled and anesthetized to the experience of my own humanity, and the humanity of others. If we are human we have, or better, we *are* this search for God, in the flesh—*in the flesh*!

Our search, however, will inevitably reveal that we are "structurally disproportionate." Even if you don't understand what these words mean, it's fun to know them anyway because you can use them to confuse people: *"Your problem, my dear man, is that you are structurally disproportionate!"* Jesus founded this tactic of making up astounding things just to confuse people, like: *"I am from above, you are from below . . ."* No wonder we read, "After that they were afraid to ask him any more questions." But back to the question at hand: "structural disproportion" means our desire is bigger than our ability to fill it. We are structured for something that we don't have and can't supply. It's like being a cup, but there's no liquid to fill it. We are that cup and we are desperately looking for water, or any liquid we can pour into it. *Anything.* And this propels our search with fierceness, because we cannot tolerate this structural disproportion: I am made for a particular fulfillment that I cannot find, but I am *going* to find it, one way or another.

So this disproportion between my thirst and my ability to quench it really is the engine of my search, of my interest. If we were content with what we could offer ourselves, we wouldn't search. This disproportion is not something negative. It's the trace of God in us. It's how God reveals the destiny for which we're created. It's how God communicates his Life to us. The divine Life has to travel through this unsatisfiable yearning. Otherwise, it doesn't penetrate to the heart. It remains added, external, and we live double lives. In this case, religion becomes a "cover-up," something we do to create a good impression, but behind closed doors we take our thirst elsewhere, or we try to shut it down. The search is so big, that if it is not preparing us to encounter the Mystery, it will prepare us to find replacements for it. And those make us slaves to finite "satisfactions." Unless . . . unless we become a search for the Infinite.

What must I do? It's the question of the Rich Young Man in the Gospel. Christianity, unlike anything else, says that if you want to find this Mystery, it's already present within this world. Look inside your own humanity, look deeper into it, because the Mystery was made flesh. The Mystery entered this world and is seducing me in every drop of rain that falls. You begin to see that this is the true nature of reality: its symbolic capacity, its "sacramentality"—beauty is seducing us, and without clinging to the finite, we must allow it to inspire our yearning for the Infinite, Beauty with a capital *B*. This is the process of conversion. *What must I do?* I must be overcome by beauty, by beautiful things, by finding beauty everywhere. Life is not easy. Sometimes we panic. But through it all, there is this haunting seduction process. Don't oppose it. Allow yourself to be wooed by beauty, overwhelmed by beauty. This is what it's all about.

But again, the question comes, *What must I do?* Really, I tell you, hang loose, let it happen. Suddenly, you are being seduced. *You* are being seduced. Seduction in general is an abstraction. Each one of us is an unrepeatable *person*. One doesn't seduce in general. One seduces in a very particular way. It is *you* who are being seduced by Christ, by the Trinity, by God. It's awesome. And it's already happening. Allow yourself to be overwhelmed by the tenderness of the Nazarene—the tender stretching of your mind, of your heart, to dimensions you never thought possible. It can be painful, a little bit scary, and we can be tempted to close the doors to it. But if you are simple in your spirit, poor of heart, you will detect something inexpressible, something for which there is no substitute, something you cannot manufacture . . . a gift, a grace. It's pure and simple wonder. Everything is grace. Everything is gift. Everything is beautiful. At this point you are seeing reality as it is: everything is *sacramental* . . . everything is a sign of the Infinite.

To the degree that we see sacramentally, we desire to live sacramentally. The giving to others of what does not come from us is called "sacrament" in the language of the Church: I give what I, in myself, do not have to give, what I've received in my structural disproportion. Having received, I am now sent on a mission. The word "Mass" comes from this word *missio*. For, having received the sacrament of all we desire, we are sent: "Go and announce the Gospel of the Lord" to others who are also structurally disproportionate. They will thank you. Or, maybe, crucify you. But woe to us if we do not share what we have been given!

ACKNOWLEDGMENTS

I owe a debt of gratitude to the many thinkers from whom I have drawn throughout this work, but especially to the following: Karol Wojtyla/Pope John Paul II, Joseph Ratzinger/Pope Benedict XVI, Monsignor Lorenzo Albacete, and Dr. Timothy Patitsas. The theological wisdom of these four men played an essential role in helping me formulate these meditations.

My dear friend and colleague Bill Howard worked tirelessly to bring this book from initial manuscript to final printed product, and Sherry Russell showed great patience with me even when I introduced various changes after her fine work typesetting the manuscript. Special thanks goes to my daughter, Beth, for providing both the cover and the interior art. I am also grateful to the following men and women who read various drafts of the manuscript and offered valuable feedback: Dr. Christine Dalessio, Fr. Ryan Mann, Fr. Patrick Schultz, Brandon Vogt, Cindy Costello, Jeanette Clark, Patrick Reidy, John Henry Gray, and Bonnie West. Finally, I couldn't do the work I do without the excellent ministry team at the Theology of the Body Institute. I'm especially grateful to Jason Clark for his dedication to the common mission we share.

Christopher West's passion for the sacramentality of beauty (how finite beauty points to infinite Beauty) has led to a prolific career as a Catholic theologian, best-selling author, and global lecturer devoted to helping others "see" and encounter the divine mystery as it is revealed in and through our physical world, especially the human body. Dr. West serves as president of the Theology of the Body Institute near Philadelphia and as Professor of Theological Anthropology in its jointly sponsored master's program with Pontifex University. His work has been featured in *The New York Times*, on ABC News, Fox News, MSNBC, and in countless Catholic and evangelical media outlets. Of all his titles and accomplishments, West is most proud to call himself a devoted husband and father. He and Wendy have enjoyed raising their five children in an historic log home surrounded by the woods and Amish farms of Lancaster County, Pennsylvania.

CONTINUE YOUR JOURNEY AT

EATINGTHESUNRISE.COM

- Sign up to receive a bonus chapter on the link between sexual and liturgical chaos.

- Learn about other resources and opportunities that will help you dive more deeply into *Eating the Sunrise*.

Dive Deeper into Theology of the Body!

Join the thousands of men and women from around the world whose lives have been transformed by our **TOB1 Online Course!**

Learn more about our TOB1 Online Course and our many other courses at **TOBINSTITUTE.ORG/COURSES**

PROVIDING RESOURCES
FOR LIFE'S BURNING QUESTIONS

BEST SELLING BOOKS

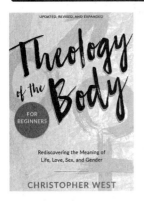

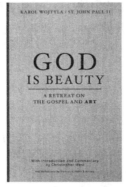

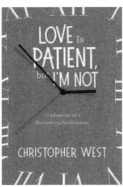

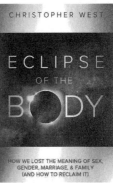

STUDY PROGRAMS

SHOP AT TOBINSTITUTE.SHOP

WE INVITE YOU TO
JOIN OUR PATRON COMMUNITY

PATRON COMMUNITY

*THE TOB **PATRON** COMMUNITY GATHERS ENTHUSIASTS FROM AROUND THE WORLD WHO WANT TO LIVE, LEARN AND SHARE ST. JOHN PAUL II'S THEOLOGY OF THE BODY. IN ADDITION TO SUPPORTING THE GLOBAL WORKS OF THE INSTITUTE, PATRONS HAVE ACCESS TO EXCLUSIVE FORMATION AND OTHER GREAT PERKS!*

AS A **PATRON**

- *YOU MAKE OUR WORK POSSIBLE.*
- *YOU ARE PART OF A COMMUNITY*
- *YOU ARE A DEFENDER OF TRUTH.*
- *YOU ARE A GIFT TO US.*

OUR **GIFT TO YOU**

- *VAST LIBRARY OF VIDEOS & AUDIO TALKS*
- *ONLINE STUDY PROGRAMS*
- *EXCLUSIVE VIRTUAL RETREATS*
- *VIRTUAL PILGRIMAGES*
- *PAST VIRTUAL CONFERENCES*

BECOME A PATRON AT
TOBPATRON.COM

MADE FOR MORE

VISIONS OF THE PROMISED LAND

with
CHRISTOPHER **WEST**   *MUSIC BY* MIKE **MANGIONE**

Join Christopher West and Mike Mangione as they creatively weave together dynamic presentations with live music, video clips, and sacred art for an evening of beauty and reflection on the meaning of life, love, and human destiny. You will come away with a faith-filled vision of hope that will instill in you the sheer wonder and joy of being alive...

BRING MADE FOR MORE TO YOUR AREA

VISIT *TOBINSTITUTE.ORG/LIVE-EVENTS*

JOIN US ON AN UPCOMING
PILGRIMAGE

Here's what you'll get when you join a

Theology of the Body Institute Pilgrimage:

– **FORMATION** *FROM DR. CHRISTOPHER WEST & TOB INSTITUTE TEAM* –

– **DAILY MASS, CONFESSION** & **SPIRITUAL DIRECTION** –

– *EXCELLENT* **HOTELS** & **RESTAURANTS** –

– **FREE TIME** *TO EXPLORE* –

– *IMMERSION INTO* **LOCAL CULTURE** –

– *A FUN* **PILGRIM FAMILY** –

– *AND* **SO MUCH MORE** –

FOR MORE INFORMATION, VISIT *TOBPILGRIMAGES.COM*